UN**BROKEN**

UNBROKEN

8 ENDURING PROMISES GOD WILL KEEP

JEFF VINES

Standard®
PUBLISHING

Cincinnati, Ohio

Published by Standard Publishing, Cincinnati, Ohio

www.standardpub.com

Copyright © 2012 Standard Publishing

Also available: *Unbroken Group Member Discussion Guide,* ISBN 978-0-7847-3309-7, copyright © 2012 by Standard Publishing.

Printed in: United States of America

Acquisitions editor: Dale Reeves

Cover design: Scott Lee Designs

Interior design: Dina Sorn at Ahaa! Design

ISBN 978-0-7847-3308-0

       Library of Congress Cataloging-in-Publication Data

Vines, Jeff.
   Unbroken : 8 enduring promises God will keep / Jeff Vines.
     p. cm.
   Includes bibliographical references (p.   ).
   ISBN 978-0-7847-3308-0
   1. Christian life. 2. God--Promises--Biblical teaching. I. Title.
   BV4509.5.V56 2012
   231.7--dc23
                      2011043008

17 16 15 14 13 12   1 2 3 4 5 6 7 8 9

∞

ACKNOWLEDGMENTS

No work of this nature comes solely from one person's gifts, talents, and abilities. Rather, God brings a group of people together to accomplish a common goal—as he so often does with the church of Jesus Christ.

I owe a debt of gratitude to the editors at Standard Publishing for their tireless efforts to keep me on track and on time. Melding their desires with my writing style has been a challenging and enjoyable experience.

Without Robin Lommori's research and documentation work, this book never would have gone to print. Thanks, Robin.

I also would like to thank Christ's Church of the Valley, and more specifically, Dana Erickson, my executive pastor, for creating the necessary space for me to be able to complete this project.

And finally, as always, I want to thank my wife, Robin; my daughter, Sian; and my son, Delaney. Without their encouragement and support, none of this ever would have become a reality.

CONTENTS

INTRODUCTION

WHEN I WAS A boy, my father asked me to stand on a chair and fall backwards into his arms. Perceiving my hesitation, he assured me I could trust him—he promised to catch me. Finally, I fell, and sure enough, he caught me. Then he looked straight into my eyes and said, "Son, you can always trust that your father will keep his promises."

My friend learned a lesson from his father too. His father asked him to sit on a chair and then lean backwards into the chair until the chair tipped over. The father promised to catch him before any damage could be done. My friend, incredibly cautious, was not easily persuaded. But after much prodding and coercing, he finally leaned back in the chair. He crashed onto the hardwood floor, receiving minor cuts and bruises to his back and shoulders. The father looked into the eyes of his son and said, "Let this be a lesson to you. Trust no one!"

Promises made to children are of paramount importance. If our parents assure us that Santa will bring us a bicycle, the Tooth Fairy will bring us cash, or the Easter Bunny will bring us chocolate, we expect the promise to be kept. Our parents said it, so it must be true. Children need to know that they can believe the people they most love and respect. Unfortunately, many adults do not keep their word—to children or other adults either.

And so the second lesson above, rather than the first, illustrates the manner in which we see the world: "Trust no one!" A person's word or promise does not hold the power it once did. A handshake is no longer enough; there must be a contract. A man's word is no longer sufficient; there must be a signed and witnessed agreement. Marriage vows are no longer complete; there must be a prenuptial agreement. Taking a person at his word is seen by many to be downright foolish.

When hopeful politicians gear up for the next election, a tsunami of promises rushes at us. But we've learned to steel ourselves against election-year vows. Promises are easy to make but sometimes difficult—and often impossible—to keep.

Yes, we feel the impact of an "over-promise, under-deliver" society. We witness the coercive propaganda of politicians, the greed and manipulation of high-powered business executives, and the exposed failures of celebrity heroes . . . sometimes all in a single day! To make matters worse, we've even seen duplicity in the lives of Christian leaders. Some of my young friends here in Los Angeles have begun to wonder whether any real difference exists between the secular and Christian world. The question really matters to them. They are desperately looking for someone they can believe in.

This book is about the One whose promises endure and *can* always be trusted, whose commitments *are* always kept, whose Word *is* always true. Jesus said, "I am the . . . truth" (John 14:6). John, Jesus' disciple, categorically claimed that God's Word is truth (John 17:17). Jesus said that not even the smallest part of any letter of any word recorded in the law of God would pass away without total fulfillment (Matthew 5:18). In John 8:31, 32, Jesus said that his teaching is true and that this truth has the power to set us free.

Freedom. Freedom from worry and fear. Freedom from meaninglessness and purposelessness. Freedom from the doubt that plagues the human race—that we are alone, that this is it, that we are nothing more than an accidental grouping of chemicals adrift on the sea of random processes and destined to return to the dust of the earth. The same Jesus who said that he was the truth also said that he was the life (John 14:6), and he promises us freedom from our own sin, eternal life to those who trust his Word and believe in him (John 3:15, 16).

> This book is about the One whose promises endure and *can* always be trusted, whose commitments *are* always kept, whose Word *is* always true.

In other words, Jesus' promises are associated with the things that really matter! Promising to catch me when I fall from a chair is one thing, but promising to forgive me, save me, and give me what I really need is another thing entirely. Promising to lower taxes or increase health care is one thing, but making a commitment to come alongside me when I desperately need help, care for me in the darkest times of my life, and answer when I call out from the pit of despair . . . that's life-changing stuff!

Those are exactly the types of promises and commitments Jesus makes. And our willingness to count on his promises dramatically changes the manner in which we see the events of our lives.

When I wrote this introduction, I was in the Atlanta airport awaiting a flight home after attending the funeral of my father. When my mother died unexpectedly just a few years ago, my heart was torn in two, and the presence of my father was a genuine consolation. Now with my father gone, I feel as if I have drifted far from home and do not know the way back. Overwhelming sadness and a myriad of other emotions have taken me on a roller-coaster ride through the valley of the shadow of death. Already prone to depression, I have felt myself teetering on the edge of a real collapse.

And yet, through it all, the promises of God that both my mother and father drilled into my emotional constitution have come to the surface to sustain me. These promises hold me up when all strength is gone. They symbolically grab my collar and drag me to what is real and true.

As we lowered my dad's casket into the ground, I continued to hear the promise Jesus gave to Mary and Martha, the sisters of Lazarus: "I am the resurrection and the life. The one who believes in me will live, even though they die; and whoever lives by believing in me will never die" (John 11:25, 26). As the Holy Spirit activates the right word at the right time, my spirits are lifted as the world turns upright again. The reminder that God's promises are true, and that he can be trusted to keep his Word in every situation, turns my mourning into dancing. My praise intensifies for the One whose promises endure.

For every fundamental need in human existence there is a corresponding promise from God that directly applies to that need. Therefore, it is my hope and prayer that as you read this book, you will learn (or rediscover) a foundational lesson: You can always trust that your Father will keep his promises! God's promises are now, and will remain, unbroken.

CHAPTER ONE

I WILL
BE WITH YOU
DANIEL 3:1, 4-28

HOW DO YOU RESPOND to life's worst-case scenarios? What do you do when your boss tells you that your services are no longer needed, when a trusted and valued relationship comes to an abrupt end, when your hopes and dreams are shattered, when you realize that something for which you had sincerely prayed will never become reality?

In the present economic crisis, many of my friends are indeed facing their worst-case scenarios. They have invested countless hours in the same job for twenty, thirty, or even forty years. Golfing, fishing, traveling, and everything that was part and parcel to retirement seemed imminent. Yet in a matter of moments, a volatile market came crashing down, and just like that—in an instant—everything changed. Investments gone! Fortunes altered! Worst-case scenarios realized!

I recently turned forty-five years old. According to statistics, I am halfway to death (what a pleasant thought!). I guess I knew that already—some of my classmates are already gone. But for the first time I have begun to contemplate the fragility of life. Not too long ago I was on the couch in the green room, waiting to preach the first of the seven services we do every weekend at Christ's Church of the Valley in San Dimas, California. My heart began pounding at an unusually rapid pace. I felt that at any moment I was going to pass out. Having lost my mother to a heart attack a few years earlier, I braced myself for the worst-case scenario!

I learned a huge lesson that day: you can't drink five diet Mountain Dews and expect no repercussions from the caffeine. Some worst-case scenarios we bring on ourselves!

The astounding truth about worst-case scenarios is that some people don't seem to be fazed by them, which is mind-boggling, if you ask me. When I started writing this chapter, I was in New Zealand. Just the night before, I had spoken to a packed house on the topic "God and Earthquakes" (in response to the 6.3M earthquake in Christchurch, New Zealand, in February 2011). When I agreed to go to New Zealand, I expected to find nothing but death, devastation, and anger toward God. While much of that was indeed present, I kept running into people whose faith and trust in God had not been deterred by even the smallest degree. How can we explain this? Why do some people not merely survive earthquakes and worst-case scenarios but, in fact, thrive in those times?

SURVIVING MOUNTAIN LIONS **AND OTHER THINGS**

I am blessed to have a group of leaders at my church who understand the importance of refilling your bucket from time to time. When I am running on empty, the elders grant me a few weeks to read and pray. On my last "bucket break," I bought a book called *The Worst-Case Scenario Survival Handbook.*[1]

> I kept running into people whose faith and trust in God had not been deterred by even the smallest degree.

The book was not exactly life-changing. In fact, most of the chapters were irrelevant. One chapter explained how to escape from quicksand; I can't imagine ever needing to know how to escape from quicksand. And surely I'll never have to wrestle myself free from an alligator or land a plane. Why would I possibly need to learn how to jump from a building into a dumpster? Or how to perform a tracheotomy . . . with a ballpoint pen! Really?

Some of the advice in the book was quite predictable, like the chapter on how to deal with a charging bull. Rule number one: Do not antagonize the bull. I guess that means you don't say, "Hey, you stupid bull!" That's not smart!

Other chapters left too many unanswered questions. If you jump out of an airplane and your parachute doesn't open, what do you do? First, signal to your jumping partner.

Well, what happens if you don't have a jumping partner?

Second, get your jumping partner to lock arms with you.

But what if your jumping partner is not experienced with this? You will likely break your arms and legs, but at least you will both survive, which is all well and good for you, but what about the guy whose parachute was going to open properly? Now he potentially has two broken arms and two broken legs!

> No matter how rough the seas, how distant the shore, how violent the wind . . . you and I will never be torn from our Creator's moorings.

There's a park near my house where I like to take my dog for a run. (OK, my dog takes me.) I've heard there are mountain lions here in California, and so when I'm running in the evening on the back side of this huge park, the seclusion begins to get a little eerie—the perfect place for a mountain lion to emerge. I often wonder, *If a mountain lion jumped out right now, could I survive that? What would I do? How would I react?* I would not necessarily have to outrun the mountain lion—I would just have to outrun my dog, right?

Well, that book removes all doubt and allows me to face this worst-case scenario with some certainty. When you face a mountain lion, what should you do? Here are your options:

A. Run.
B. Play dead.
C. Make yourself look bigger by opening your coat.
D. Sing a gentle, happy song.

Before I had read the book, I would have chosen B, play dead. I know that running would never work. That seems to play right into the lion's hand; prey always runs! Singing seems ridiculous and opening your coat seems futile, but playing dead—although difficult to do when your heart is beating out of your chest—seemed the most logical choice. Logical as it may seem, it's the wrong answer. The answer is actually to open your coat and make yourself look bigger. But here's the problem: we don't wear coats in California, which is why mountain lions are killing us!

The book promised to prepare me to survive any eventuality, but I had doubts. I wasn't able to put full confidence in it. I want a guarantee. I need promises I can count on.

THE CERTAINTY OF **GOD'S PROMISES**

One of the most encouraging passages in the New Testament concerns Jesus' promise to his disciples that he would be with them and would never leave them (see Matthew 28:20; John 15:4). No matter how rough the seas, how distant the shore, how violent the wind . . . you and I will never be torn from our Creator's moorings. But what exactly does that mean? Will God, at the first sign of trouble, provide a secret door through which we can escape? Is Jesus implying that no trouble will ever come our way?

If we are honest, that is the scenario most of us want. I want a life that never needs a parachute! I want a life void of mountain lions. And if the mountain lion does appear, I want God to take him behind the woodshed and smack him around a little bit and warn him about the consequences of messing with a child of God! Yes! That's what I want: instantaneous deliverance from trouble! However, the biblical narrative seems to portray a different kind of God—not a God who delivers *from* trouble, but a God who delivers *through* trouble.

Therefore, when tragic situations arise—and knowing that God is alive and well—how are we who are Christians to respond? How do we respond to worst-case scenarios? I believe that Daniel 3 answers that question.

AN UNPREDICTABLE **KING**

King Nebuchadnezzar made an image of gold, sixty cubits high and six cubits wide [*that's approximately ninety feet tall and nine feet wide*], and set it up on the plain of Dura in the province of Babylon. He then summoned the satraps, prefects, governors, advisers, treasurers, judges, magistrates and all the other provincial officials to come to the dedication of the image he had set up. So the satraps, prefects, governors, advisers, treasurers, judges, magistrates and all the other provincial officials assembled for the dedication of the image that King Nebuchadnezzar had set up, and they stood before it.

Then the herald loudly proclaimed, "Nations and peoples of every language, this is what you are commanded to do: As soon as you hear the sound of the horn, flute, zither, lyre, harp, pipe and all kinds of music, you must fall down and worship the image of gold that King Nebuchadnezzar has set up. Whoever does not fall down and worship will immediately be thrown into a blazing furnace."

Therefore, as soon as they heard the sound of the horn, flute, zither, lyre, harp and all kinds of music, all the nations and peoples of every language fell down and worshiped the image of gold that King Nebuchadnezzar had set up (Daniel 3:1-7).

King Nebuchadnezzar, although super intelligent, was notorious for knee-jerk reactions void of wisdom. In fact, King Neb was the epitome of contradiction. On the one hand he reeked of intelligence. When Babylon conquered the surrounding nations, rather than annihilating their leaders, he preserved those with great wisdom and leadership skills, escorted them into the palace, and made them part of his brain trust. He would take the wisest of the wise among every nation and place them into government positions. This tactic significantly increased the IQ of his personal cabinet as well as catalyzed peace throughout the empire. Every conquered nation felt that in some small way they were represented. Yet things were about to come crumbling down.

Back in Daniel 2, King Nebuchadnezzar had the most fascinating dream. He saw a rather daunting statue featuring a head of gold, chest and arms of silver, belly and thighs of bronze, legs of iron, and feet of clay. Desperate to understand the meaning of the dream, he called a cabinet meeting and demanded that the wise men interpret his dream. I imagine that the conversation went something like this:

King Neb: Hey guys! I had this dream. Tell me what it means.

Wise men: Yes, great king. Tell us what you dreamed, and then we will tell you what it means.

King Neb: Oh no. I'm not falling for that! If you really have a special gift of seeing what others cannot see, then you should be able to tell me not only the meaning of the dream, but the dream itself. [*This is a wise king!*]

Wise men: Oh, king! No man can do that! This is not fair! What you ask is unreasonable! No wise man has ever been asked to do such a thing!

King Neb: Is that your final answer?

Wise men: Um . . .

King Neb (to his guards): Kill them! Kill them all!

Wow! Kill all the wise men? That is not what the wise men expected. A close reading of the text reveals that King Neb was so furious that he was going to eradicate not only those present, but all the wise men in all of Babylon! This is where Daniel, Shadrach, Meshach, and Abednego entered the story. As Hebrews conquered by Babylon and recruited by the king to live in the "wise man palace," these young men fell under the wrath of the king's edict. Word of the scheduled eradication of all the wise men reached Daniel, and he immediately sent an urgent message to the king: "There is a God in heaven who reveals mysteries" (2:28). Daniel essentially said to the king, "No man can do what you're asking, but my God in Heaven can."

> King Neb was so furious that he was going to eradicate not only those present, but all the wise men in all of Babylon!

Impressed, the king extended a personal invitation to Daniel. Daniel traveled to the palace and took care of business. With uncanny precision he related both the dream and its interpretation. Thrilled and relieved, the king emphatically claimed, "Surely your God is the God of gods and the Lord of kings and a revealer of mysteries" (v. 47).

Unfortunately, Nebuchadnezzar had a very short memory. His praise of the true God, Yahweh, soon dissolved in favor of a new program of self-aggrandizement.

OK, let's be honest. We're the same way! The divide between King Neb and us is not very wide. As long as God gives us what we want, praise and worship come easy, right? When he gives us the job we've always wanted, the house of our dreams, or the girl for whom we have prayed, then it is easy to say, "Surely, God is the God of gods!" When we get what we want, we are happy people. Unfortunately, even though the king heard the interpretation of the dream, he missed its primary significance. Daniel had just told him: "You, O king, are the head of gold. Your kingdom will become great, but your kingdom will not last. (Clay feet, you know.) In fact, three other kingdoms will come and go, and then a kingdom, an unshakable kingdom, will usher in a new age that will last forever" (vv. 36-45, my paraphrase).

IT'S ALL ABOUT MOTIVE

You would think that Nebuchadnezzar would ask more questions concerning the unshakable kingdom that was to come. Instead he was fixated on the feet of clay. Rather than being enthralled with the kingdom of all kingdoms, he was worried about his own kingdom. We can almost hear him, deep in thought, as he imagines the feet of clay: *That's why my kingdom's not going to last. It has a weak foundation—the feet are made of clay. That's the problem, so I've got to make my kingdom strong! But why is my kingdom weak? I know, because it's not unified! We're different people groups from different cultures. I need to come up with a plan that will unify the people . . . I've got it! One religion will surely do the trick!*

So the king erected a statue that stood ninety feet high! It was immense, it was expensive, it was intimidating! In an attempt to force the issue, he announced another edict (through his herald): "Here's what I want you to do: The band is going to play all these different instruments in an effort to ensure that there's at least one sound with which a person can identify. Everyone will go out of Babylon to the plains of Dura. The leaders will be seated before all the people, and we're all going to gather around and bow down to this intimidating statue" (3:4, 5, my paraphrase).

The message was simple: bow or die!

So a sea of thousands of people flowed into the plains of Dura. Have you ever been to the opening ceremony of the Olympics? People who've been there tell me that it triggers a sensation like no other. You feel powerful and invincible. There is an electricity in the air as all those people and cultures flow into the stadium for one unified purpose. This is the feeling the king was trying to create.

Remember, the king's main concerns weren't really about religion. The statue may have represented himself, his patron god, or just the worship of any god of choice. Many commentators believe that King Neb was looking for political glue that would unify the kingdom and solidify its foundation. Because he attributed no name to the statue, people could name the god whatever they wanted—that was their prerogative. What better way to elicit everyone's pledge of loyalty to the state than with a rousing ceremony!

However, there was one nonnegotiable—everyone had to bow when the music played. The message was simple: bow or die!

THE YOUNG MEN **TAKE A STAND**

Picture King Nebuchadnezzar's rage when three young Hebrew men refused to comply. One could easily imagine that as soon as the music began—*BOOM*—everybody dropped to the ground. But pretty quickly, everyone's attention moved from the statue to these three, who obviously possessed a fiery-furnace death wish. Worse yet, these were not just three average Joes; these were three of the most powerful men in the kingdom—Shadrach, Meshach, and Abednego (see 2:49).

Daniel 3:8 says, "At this time some astrologers came forward and denounced the Jews." The Hebrew word for *denounced* used in this text means "to devour," as when an animal eats the pieces of its prey.[2] There's extreme hostility here. Motivated by professional jealousy, intense racism, and a revengeful spirit, the wise men who had been unable to interpret the king's dream could not believe the opportunity that had fallen into their laps. Surely Daniel's friends were going to die! I imagine the conversation (in 3:14, 15) going something like this:

King Neb: Is it true, boys? After all I have given you, you refused to bow down?

S-M-A (Shadrach, Meshach, and Abednego): Yes, O king. We did not bow down to the idol.

King Neb: Now boys, you know that I value you and your friend Daniel. Ordinarily, I would have just thrown you guys into the furnace, but I really, really, like you. So I want to give you one more chance, OK?

S-M-A: OK.

King Neb: Now, you know the rule, right? The music plays and you drop. But if you do not drop and worship, you will be thrown immediately into a blazing furnace. And boys, what god will be able to rescue you then?

Nebuchadnezzar's question was rhetorical. He was not looking for information! When I was a child, my mother used to ask me those types of questions on a regular basis:

- "Do you want a spanking?"
- "Do you want me to ground you?"
- "Do you want me to call your father?"
- "Do you want me to come down there?"

Those were not questions; they were threats! King Nebuchadnezzar was saying, "You'd better understand something! There's no escape. There's no way out. Obey me or else!"

OUR GOD **IS ABLE**

When I lived as a missionary in Zimbabwe, Africa, the little children of the Shona tribe loved to stand up at Vacation Bible School, put their arms into the air, flex their muscles, and sing, "My God is so big, so strong and so mighty, there's nothing my God cannot do!"[3] By itself, the song was powerful enough, but when the children flexed their muscles, the song seemed to morph into a superman-like melody that left little doubt in even the strongest of skeptics that God was indeed POWERFUL!

The fact that God is *able* brings mental tension into unfortunate situations where we expect God to deliver us from evil. Yes, we know God is able, but is he willing? If he is, terrific! If he is not, then why not? The biblical narrative constantly reminds us that God is with us, but it never guarantees an escape hatch from trouble or the kind of miraculous intervention that prevents an oncoming storm.

Yes, he is able!

Yes, he is strong!

Yes, he is mighty!

But he is also sovereign and is always bringing his plan to fruition. More importantly, the Bible reminds us that history is God's story. Our lives are ultimately about what God is doing in the world. As difficult as it might be for many to embrace, it's not about what we want; it's about God.

Shadrach, Meshach, and Abednego understood this. When they first heard the edict that had been passed, they must have known that outside of God's intervention, death was imminent. I believe that they met together long before the exodus to the plains of Dura. They held each other accountable and agreed that there was no way they were going to bow down to this false idol, despite the worst-case scenario (the fiery furnace). I believe they prayed that the edict would never pass. But it passed. I think they prayed that Nebuchadnezzar would repent after the edict had been passed. But he did not repent. Maybe they prayed that the king, knowing the integrity of their faith and the monotheistic belief of the Hebrews, would excuse them from the ceremony. But they received no permission to be excused. Maybe they prayed that no one would notice their abstention. But someone noticed. Maybe they prayed that those who noticed would keep quiet. But they did not keep quiet. All their prayers were answered, but the answer was always no.

BUT EVEN IF **HE DOES NOT** . . .

As a result of their obedience, Shadrach, Meshach, and Abednego were facing a worst-case scenario. Every escape route had been blocked. The parachute was not opening; they were locking arms with each other and falling at a rapid pace. And then Nebuchadnezzar offered one more chance, but these young men weren't backing down. They were serious about their God, and so they responded in a bold and courageous way: "King Nebuchadnezzar, we do not need to defend ourselves before you in this matter. If we are thrown into the blazing furnace, the God we serve is able to deliver us from it, and he will deliver us from Your Majesty's hand" (3:16, 17).

> The fact that God is *able* brings mental tension into unfortunate situations where we expect God to deliver us from evil.

In other words, "King Neb, you asked us earlier who is able to save us from your hand. Here is your answer: YAHWEH! The God of our fathers Abraham, Isaac, and Jacob! He is able!"

Every time I read that passage I want to shout, "Yes! You'd better watch out, king! Don't make God come down there! You have no idea who you are messing with! Our God is able!" But then the next line comes: "But even if he does not, we want you to know, Your Majesty, that we will not serve your gods or worship the image of gold you have set up" (v. 18). These young men had already decided that even in the face of their worst-case scenario, they would not turn their backs on God.

ON WHAT DOES **YOUR FAITH DEPEND?**

Where worst-case scenarios are concerned, there is a valuable lesson to be learned. If you wait until the trouble is upon you to decide the manner in which you will respond to it, you will most often choose the easy way out. However, the easy way out is not always the best and, in fact, in the long run may not be that easy after all.

On one of my recent speaking trips to New Zealand, I was on my way to the hotel fitness center when I came across a poster of Muhammad Ali in his training attire, throwing a right hook at the punching bag. The caption at the bottom read, "The fight is won or lost far away from witnesses—behind the lines, in the gym, and out there on the road, long before I dance under those lights."[4]

The fight is won long before the battle begins.

The fact is, God is with us before, during, and after the trouble comes our way. He is with us *before* in the sense that his Spirit is building within us the character and integrity essential to do the right thing even under extreme conditions. He is with us *during* the tragedy by never calling us to endure something without assuming the responsibility to equip us to endure it. And he is with us *after* the struggle by reminding us once again that his strength is sufficient for us in all things. "The eyes of the LORD range throughout the earth to strengthen those whose hearts are fully committed to him" (2 Chronicles 16:9).

Shadrach, Meshach, and Abednego had won the fight long before the battle began. Their faith and commitment to God were not contingent on any external circumstance. Like Job who said, "Though he slay me, yet will I hope in him" (Job 13:15), these young men maintained an attitude that exclaimed, "Even if God does not deliver us and even if we burn in the fire, we're still not going to worship, serve, or bow down to your god, King Nebuchadnezzar!"

Ask yourself: "On what does my faith in God depend? Are there conditions?"

> The fact is, God is with us before, during,
> and after the trouble comes our way.

All too often my conversation with God tends to go something like this: "O God, if you will just do this one thing, then I'll do this for you." Too many times we say, "If you will get me the promotion, if you'll heal my disease, if you'll save my child . . . then . . ." People often come to me believing that my pastoral prayers are more powerful than those of the "average" Christian. They say to me, "Pastor Jeff, if God will do this one thing for me, then I will go to church every week (or start tithing or serve in the children's ministry or . . .)." When God fails to deliver as they expect him to, they often cry out, "Where are you, God?"

Is your faith in God based on any conditions? What would have to happen to finally make you say, "All right, God, I was with you up to this point, but now I'm out. I'm leaving. I have come this far, but I can't go any farther." When you come to that line, that's when you will discover the idol, or false god, in your life.

During my university days I became rather close to one of my professors. A gifted teacher and passionate Christian, he looked just like Moses—or at least what I always envisioned Moses looking like: white beard, white hair, and spiritual disposition. For many of the students, he became the benchmark for Christian faith. WWPD (What Would Professor Do?) became a popular motto. Before you walked into his classroom, you almost felt compelled to remove your shoes to approach this holy ground.

Now if anyone's faith appeared unshakable, it was his. Surely nothing could destroy such strong and mighty faith. To my professor, God was all—his life, his being, his hope, his rock, his fortress . . . everything. God was the love of his life. Nothing and no one would ever deter his praise, worship, and trust toward God.

When we received the news that the professor's granddaughter had been diagnosed with leukemia, our hearts ached. This man loved his granddaughter like no other grandfather I have known. It is true that those who love God most are able to love people most. Love for God comes as a result of understanding the depth of God's love for us. When we understand the overwhelming mercy and grace God grants us, we tend to extend that same grace and mercy to others, and our love for people grows with our love for God.

Consistent with the professor's life of faith, he invited students to join him in prayer for the healing of his granddaughter. As this journey of prayer intensified, it became clear that the professor truly believed that God was going to provide the miracle. He could often be overheard saying, "I am already praising God for the healing he's going to bring." With each passing week, the intensity of his prayers was outweighed only by the certainty of his faith. "God will heal my granddaughter," he proclaimed.

When his granddaughter died, we watched as the man we had known became a shadow of his former self. He began to withdraw from the students. The once jovial, outgoing, determined man of faith seemed to lose all hope and trust in a sovereign God. Many of the students tried to understand the sadness and ache in his heart, but we also thought that in time, the healing would come and after he endured this experience in the valley, he would soon find himself on the mountaintop again.

But the recovery never seemed to come. His faith had truly been shaken, and he had lost his spiritual thirst. God seemed distant to him in the later years of his life. Theologians speak of *deus absconditus*—the hidden God—and it seemed that in the professor's thinking, God had hidden too well and perhaps was not worthy of being found.

I cannot be certain that my professor ever made his peace with God, but I do know that there are things that can change a man. Seeing such things has taught me never to judge that person but to instead ask myself, "On what does *my* faith depend?" My greatest fear is that something would happen to one of my children. And if that were to happen, how would my view of God change? Or would it?

Young women say to me, "You know, Jeff, I want a husband so bad. I don't understand why God hasn't brought a man into my life." If a woman who says words like those believes that she can be happy only if she is married, she has allowed those desires to become more important than trusting that her joy will come from the Lord. If her desire for a man is greater than her love for God, those desires have become an idol in her life.

I used to think that God would surely provide the right man in the right time for such women, but what if God does not provide a man? What if a woman honors God, loses the man she's having second thoughts about, and another one doesn't come along? Is her faith and trust in God contingent on how God does or does not deliver?

ANSWERING **THE WHY**

Yes, I know that the Bible says, "We know that in all things God works for the good of those who love him, who have been called according to his purpose" (Romans 8:28). I am aware that we are reminded just a few verses later that no outside force can separate us from God's love (vv. 38, 39). However, early in my Christian journey, I became frustrated with the fact that the Bible gives very few answers concerning the why, when it comes to our tragedies. But there are many people who could better endure the *what* if they knew the *why*—at least, that's the conventional wisdom. Job's story is a reminder of the manner in which God works. I find Job's story to be the most helpful piece of literature one could ever read during difficult times.

For thirty-some chapters Job questioned God about the reason for the sufferings he was enduring. The writer clearly expresses that Job was a "blameless and upright man" (Job 1:1), leaving us to assume that Job's calamity was not the result of discipline or sin. As Job's trials piled up, the Scripture tells us that Job did not sin in response (1:22; 2:10). And even during Job's intense questioning of God, Job's righteousness is highlighted (13:23 and 31:33, for example). I take that to mean that God isn't offended at our questions. And after all, Job *was* continuing to resolve his dilemma within the context of God.

If we exist on this planet as a result of time plus matter plus chance, as atheistic evolution claims, life is not sacred, and intrinsic worth is merely a hope and dream. Moreover, pain is merely the ultimate expression of a world that is ridding itself of the weak so that the strong may survive. So asking questions about why someone has to suffer implies that you place a value on human life—that there is something wrong about a person's getting destroyed or being made to experience pain.

> My greatest fear is that something would happen to one of my children. And if that were to happen, how would my view of God change?

After Job's persistent and passionate search for a reason for his suffering, God spoke. I can imagine the conversation going something like this:

Job: Why, God, why? Why is all this happening to me?

God: OK, Job. I have listened to your ranting and raving and have heard your voice.

Job: Good! I knew you could hear me. Are you here to respond?

God: Yes, Job, but before I respond, I want to make sure you understand what you are asking.

Job: What do you mean?

God: Well, your assumption is that if you could gain an exhaustive understanding of your pain, then you would be willing and able to endure it, right?

Job: Yes, God, that's it! If I could just understand the why, I could endure the what.

God: OK, Job, then I have a few simple questions for you . . .

And at this point, God began to paint a sweeping portrait of himself that would run for four full chapters! He showcased his power and attributes, mostly through questions like these:

- "Where were you when I laid the earth's foundation? Tell me, if you understand. Who marked off its dimensions? Surely you know! Who stretched a measuring line across it?" (Job 38:4, 5).
- "Have you journeyed to the springs of the sea or walked in the recesses of the deep?" (v. 16).
- "Have the gates of death been shown to you? Have you seen the gates of the deepest darkness?" (v. 17).
- "Can you bring forth the constellations in their seasons?" (v. 32).
- "Who gives . . . wisdom or . . . understanding?" (v. 36).
- "Do you know when the mountain goats give birth? Do you watch when the doe bears her fawn?" (39:1).

At first glance, you wonder what God is doing. However, when we place God's questions in the context of Job's struggles, a bright light appears. God is simply reminding Job that there are a thousand things that happen in Job's life every day for which he does not have an exhaustive understanding, and yet readily accepts.

Does Job understand the foundations of the world? the depths of the sea? where darkness resides? the changing of the seasons? the manner in which our brains function? how a mother goat gives birth to her young in the wilderness?

Those are fundamental properties of life that Job readily embraces without question. He knows that although he enjoys the rising and setting of the sun and possesses an elementary understanding of how that works, if he is honest with himself, there is so much more about his life that he doesn't have a clue about. Thousands of years removed from Job, we may understand two ounces of this universe, but there is still so much that we do not know.

There is a point where the finite ends and the infinite begins. In his book *Cries of the Heart,* Ravi Zacharias writes: "The immensity and specificity of the universe must humble us in the best sense of the word. The more a person knows, the more humble he or she needs to be because the entailments of knowledge remind us constantly of the vastness and intricacy of ultimate reality: the birth of a baby, the nursing of that child at its mother's breast, the boundlessness of a mother's love, the wonder of growth to maturity, the fascinating intricacy of the brain, the enchantment of human sexuality."[5]

A COMPELLING PROMISE OF HIS PRESENCE

Now if Job's story had ended there . . . in the words of my African friends,

"That would be a very sad story." But the story does not end there. We read on and discover God's promise and prevailing presence in the midst of our tragedies. Job's response to God's questions (those above and many more) is both clarifying and encouraging: "My ears had heard of you but now my eyes have seen you" (Job 42:5).

What a powerful proclamation!

Yes, it seems to us easier for people to endure suffering when they know the why. Job never did get a clear why, except that God is sovereign. What is the point? As it was when Job suffered, our pain should lead us *toward* God, not *away* from him. When we truly believe that God is sovereign and deserves our complete allegiance, we will soon discover that our pain is not just a personal problem but that we can draw nearer to God, and become more Christlike, through it.

God reveals himself in suffering and tragedy in ways you cannot know until you have traveled that road.

In my third year of ministry in Zimbabwe, I met a young, vibrant lady named Gloria. Shortly after being led to Christ, Gloria was diagnosed with cancer. Afraid that as a new believer this might shake her faith, I traveled to Bulawayo to be with her during the last few days of her life. Young and inexperienced in the ministry, I took her hand and nervously began a dissertation designed to assure her that God was still with her. Before I could complete the words of comfort I had prepared, Gloria interrupted me, "Jeff, do not worry about me. I am fine. In fact, I am better than I have ever been. God has shown me things in these last days that have brought great comfort. He has given me a little glimpse of what is to come. Thank you so much for introducing me to God. Had I not known him, I would have been unable to make it through this time."

Looking intently into her eyes I could see that something very special had happened to her. Something I honestly wish would happen to me. Then came the line I will never forget. She squeezed my hand and whispered, "Jeff, I know him in a way that you never will, until you walk the road I am presently on." With that Gloria fell asleep, and the next day she went home to be with God.

That was almost twenty years ago, and since then I have discovered that it seems to be the pattern of those who have been called on to endure such tragic circumstances. Does God reveal himself in a very special way to those whose hardships seem unbearable to the rest of us? I believe that he does.

If you are familiar with the rest of the story in Daniel 3, you are aware that God delivered the three young Hebrew men—not *from* the furnace, but *through* the furnace. In fact, had they not gone through that worst-case scenario, they would never have known what it was like to hang out with the Messiah and surf the fiery waves with the Son of God as their very own personal companion.

The Christians I have known who have suffered the most seem to know God best. In fact, they remind the rest of us of the cross and perhaps its primary message with regard to suffering: that it is quite possible to experience the worst-case scenario and at the same time be in the very center of God's will; that often God does his best work in the midst of great difficulty. Exhibit A: Jesus' sacrifice on the cross for us.

Someone may object, "But, Jeff, God abandoned Jesus when he was on the cross, and you're saying that God will be with us in our deepest trial. How can you harmonize the two?"

Jesus, in his human form, *felt* abandoned. When Jesus cried out those words of "My God, my God, why have you forsaken me?" he was echoing that sentiment David had expressed in Psalm 22:1. But just as God did not abandon David, God was not abandoning Jesus. The feeling of separation was very real, the sense of loss and grief was intense, and the pain was definitely happening. But God was still there in all of it. We must remember that when we face difficult times, God, through his Holy Spirit, is always with us. He hasn't abandoned us in the midst of our pain.

The issues surrounding pain and suffering are complex, and the answers are not easily discovered. One thing about which we can be absolutely certain is that God will be with us! We are constantly faced with the question "On what is my faith in God contingent?" And God constantly says to us, "Nothing can separate you from my love." And when we may *feel* that God has abandoned us, we must anchor our emotions in the truth: no matter how deep the waves, how strong the current, and how intimidating the storm, we will never be torn from our Creator's moorings.

And those who say, "Even if he does not . . ." may gain a glimpse of God not experienced by those who have not traveled this journey with him. They will gain a prevailing presence that gives them the strength to endure whatever God calls them to endure—because he promises he will be with them.

GREAT AND PRECIOUS PROMISES

FOR INDIVIDUAL OR GROUP STUDY

God is always with you even in the midst of your worst-case scenario. He is just as involved in your pain as he is in your pleasure. If you are walking with him and are in the Word but your life is not going according to your plan, trust that it is going according to *his* perfect plan. God's desire is not to save you *from* suffering, but to save you *through* it. Just like Job, we often think that if we knew the *why* behind our suffering, it would be easier to bear, but God is calling us to trust him even when we don't understand what's happening in our lives.

1 What does it mean to you that God does not want to save you *from* trouble, but save you *through* trouble?

2 How have you demonstrated your trust that God is always with you and is always able, even when things haven't gone your way? After coming through a rough situation or difficult phase in your life, how have you given God the glory due him like Shadrach, Meshach, and Abednego did?

3 Has there ever been a time in the midst of a difficult situation when you tried to rationalize God away, and claimed that you made it through the fiery trial on your own strength? What happened?

4 In what area of your life would you be willing to make an "even if he does not" stand for God and trust that his plan is better than yours?

5 On what does your faith depend? What kind of things happening in your life would make you question God, or decide to stop following him altogether? What is your worst-case scenario, and how do you think (or hope) you'd respond to it?

CHAPTER TWO

I WILL
CARE FOR YOU
JOHN 11:1-3, 17-44

E VERY EASTER, I'M A part of two scenarios. First, churches all over the world emphasize the triumph of good over evil, life over death, righteousness over unrighteousness. And the Bible verse "Where, O death, is your sting?" (1 Corinthians 15:55) is quoted thousands of times. Hundreds and hundreds of gifted communicators remind their audiences that no matter what happens to us in this life, God will more than make up for it in the next. And even though we may lose a few battles along the way, ultimately we will win the war! (Can you hear the hymn "Up from the Grave He Arose" in the background?)

However, the second scenario is entirely different. Every Easter students from various universities all around Southern California line up to ask me how to deal with what is taking place on their campuses. These students complain, "Pastor Jeff, my philosophy professor is challenging my faith, and I'm not sure how to respond. He's saying, 'If your Jesus is so powerful that he can conquer death, why doesn't he employ a little of that power to alleviate all the pain and suffering in our world?'"

More often, the question (which is really a statement) is phrased in this fashion: Given all the pain, suffering, and death in the world, can God really be all-powerful and all-loving at the same time? If God is all-powerful, then he would have the *ability* to wipe out all pain and suffering, and if he's all-loving (or some people say all-good), he would have the *desire* to wipe out all pain and suffering. So what's stopping him? Maybe God is not both all-powerful and all-loving. Maybe he's one or the other, but there's no way, logically speaking, he can be both.

Faulty logic is sometimes difficult to identify, but that is not the case here. Suppose I told you there was a bear in your tent. To test my statement, you could simply walk over to your tent, open the flap, and look in. If the bear is present, you would say, "Yep, I see the bear. Run, man, run!"

Haven't you ever wanted to take hold of just a little of that resurrection power to alleviate some of the pain and suffering you're struggling with?

However, if I tell you there are thousands of no-see-ums in your tent, that's a different story. Are you familiar with no-see-ums? These are actual insects (also known as biting midges). Although microscopic and extremely difficult to see (that's why they are called no-see-ums), they are a real and present pest. When you feel the bite, you know they are there! If I tell you there are no-see-ums in the tent, and you look inside to verify my statement, you wouldn't be able to see them. But that doesn't mean they're not there.

There's a point at which the finite stops and the infinite begins. To say that a good God cannot co-exist with pain and suffering assumes that there's no good reason for God ever to allow anything painful into your life or into this world. But such a position is impossible to defend. Just because you can't see the reason does not mean that a reason—and a very good one—does not exist. The bottom line is that you're not God, and thus do not possess a comprehensive knowledge of reality.

What we do know with certainty is that Jesus, as demonstrated in the resurrection, has power over all things, even death. True, we may not be able to comprehend such power, but there are times we would give anything to *apprehend* it! Haven't you ever wanted to take hold of just a little of that resurrection power to alleviate some of the pain and suffering you're struggling with?

Recently, my wife, Robin, and I were watching a PBS special highlighting the people, customs, and music of Appalachia. During one segment, we were introduced to an Appalachian farmer who had written a letter to the Oak Ridge Nuclear Power Plant. He passionately implored them to send him a small dose of this "newly discovered" nuclear power so that he could kill a skunk wreaking havoc on his property. The farmer assured the authorities that he had heard that this nuclear power was "pretty good stuff" and that he did not need all of it, just enough to "do the old rascal in."

During my twenty-six years of ministry, I have met plenty of people who desperately desire just enough of God's power to "do in" a rascal or two. I think of all the single parents who are working, struggling, and fighting to provide a hope and a future for their children. One mother said, "Pastor Jeff, you know, it's just one thing after the next! You would think God would look down, see my situation, and offer a little help from time to time." I think of all the families in financial crisis praying those same prayers: "God, help us to make it through another week, another month, another year. We're not asking for a life of luxury, just survival!"

TIME **OUT!**

Before we proceed, let's make sure we understand the issue. If we have matured in our faith, we have grown to realize that God's ways are not always understood. Relational fractures, career disasters, family struggles, physical illnesses, and emotional anxieties are all part of our human existence. Expecting God to provide an escape hatch from a world of trouble seems unrealistic. Most of our ills are either the result of our own doing or the result of someone else's freewill decision. While it is true that the freedom of having freewill opens the door to evil, pain, and suffering, on the other hand is the door that opens to love, kindness, and caring.

Most Christ followers have come to terms with the idea that having freewill means that bad things will happen (at least, they've come to terms with it in theory). The real issue for most believers concerns the question of care. Does God care? Will God care for me in the midst of all these trials? in the midst of cancer? financial disaster? divorce? depression? Moreover, in what form or shape will such care come? The thought of an all-powerful God who allows so much tragedy in life—even if those tragedies are advantageous to his accomplishing ultimate good—is difficult enough to grasp. That he might do so without tenderness, love, and care is unfathomable. So the bottom line question is: Can I really trust God? Will he be with me and care for me? Can we count on him, as Billy Graham suggested, "not only every day, but every moment of every day"?[1]

We are promised God's care: "Cast all your anxiety on him because he cares for you" (1 Peter 5:7). I believe God included the John 11 narrative in

Scripture to give us such assurance and to provide a glimpse of the manner in which he exhibits such care during the most tragic times of our lives.

IT BEGINS **WITH SICKNESS**

"Now a man named Lazarus was sick. He was from Bethany, the village of Mary and her sister Martha" (John 11:1). From the outset, we see a uniqueness in the John 11 passage. Mentioning the specific name of someone in need is not typical in the New Testament accounts. Usually, we read words like "and there was a blind man" or "there was a lame man" or "a paralyzed man" or "a man who was demon-possessed." But here, John wanted the reader to understand that this wasn't just some random guy off the street. This was Lazarus, a close, intimate friend of Jesus.

In fact, the friendship between Jesus and Lazarus was so special that when Mary and Martha sent word to Jesus to inform him of Lazarus's illness, they didn't even have to use Lazarus's name. They simply wrote, "Lord, the one you love is sick" (v. 3). Imagine being referred to in this fashion. If I, Jeff Vines, were sick, friends would tell the Lord that "the one you love" needs you, and the Lord would know they meant me! (I'm getting the warm fuzzies.)

> The thought of an all-powerful God who allows so much tragedy in life—even if those tragedies are advantageous to his accomplishing ultimate good—is difficult enough to grasp.

It seems John wrote verse 5 to prepare us for verse 6. "Now Jesus loved Martha and her sister and Lazarus." (OK, John, we got it.) But then, verse 6 seems strange in the light of verse 5: "So when [Jesus] heard that Lazarus was sick, he stayed where he was two more days" (v. 6). What? That makes little sense. A good friend drops everything when the need arises, right? When my mother died, my high school basketball coach immediately stopped what he was doing, drove to the hospital, and comforted and encouraged me for the next forty-eight hours. That is what a true friend does—he comes running in a time of need. Singer Carole King told us that years ago! "I'll come running . . . you've got a friend."[2] So what's going on here?

John 11 is a microcosm of life. God is all-powerful and all-good . . . and he was about two miles down the road from where Lazarus lived. Yet he didn't make a move. No running here. Think about it: Why did Mary and Martha call Jesus in the first place? They knew he had fed five thousand people with a little bit of food; knew he had walked on water, healed an invalid at a pool in Bethsaida, caused the lame to walk and the blind to see. In each case, Jesus did not intimately know those men, women, and children; they were mere acquaintances. But this was Lazarus, Jesus' close, close friend! You can imagine the disciples' confusion when they heard that Lazarus was ill and Jesus failed to give the command to pack up the caravan and head over the hill toward Bethany. I'm sure the disciples were thinking, *Man! Just when you think you know a guy!*

Finally, after two days of waiting, Jesus made a move. "He said to his disciples, 'Let us go back to Judea'" (v. 7). But why the delay? There's only one answer—he was waiting for Lazarus to die.

Unfortunately, Peter, James, John, and the gang—though they had fully expected Jesus to drop everything and run to Lazarus—still saw self-preservation as a greater priority than servanthood, and issued a warning. "'But Rabbi,' they said, 'a short while ago the Jews there tried to stone you, and yet you are going back?'" (v. 8). Jesus gave them a little speech about timing, then made an attempt to comfort the disciples by revealing his intentions. "After he had said this, he went on to tell them, 'Our friend Lazarus has fallen asleep; but I am going there to wake him up'" (v. 11). The disciples responded somewhat humorously: "Lord, if he sleeps, he will get better" (v. 12). In other words, "Oh, a nap is good for what ails you. If Lazarus is taking a little nap, he'll wake up later. There's no need to go back and risk our lives!"

> You can imagine the disciples' confusion when they heard that Lazarus was ill and Jesus failed to give the command to pack up the caravan and head over the hill toward Bethany.

The disciples were slow learners, so Jesus cleared the whole thing up and plainly stated: "Lazarus is dead, and for your sake I am glad I was not there, so that you may believe" (vv. 14, 15). Read that last verse with first-century eyes. *You* know how this story ends, but the disciples did not have that privilege. From their perspective, they just heard Jesus say he was glad he was not there when Lazarus died. Moreover, he said that this happened to Lazarus so that they might believe. The disciples must have been thinking, *Believe what? That you aren't a very good friend? That you're not the compassionate person we thought you were? That Lazarus and Mary and Martha needed you and you ignored them? We believe you . . .*

THE TENSION INCREASES

Mary and Martha were standing out on the road that leads to Bethany, and they knew that Jesus was only about a half hour's walk away. They stood waiting, waiting, and waiting. Hours passed. A day, a second day, a third day . . . but still, no Jesus. Mary and Martha knew precisely how long it would have taken to deliver the message to Jesus, and for Jesus to pack up the caravan and make his way back to Lazarus. In their minds, there was no doubt that Jesus would drop everything and come running. But still, no Jesus.

Maybe they reminded each other that Jesus had healed many other people, and that those other people were mere acquaintances. But this is Lazarus. Lazarus is family! You drop everything for family! So they stood out on the road, waiting and looking across the valley, hour after hour. But still, no Jesus.

And then Lazarus died.

I picture them having the funeral, and still Mary and Martha are standing out on the road, looking over their shoulders one more time, saying, "Wait! Just wait! Don't put the stone over the tomb! Wait! We know he's coming! He's got to come!" But still, no Jesus. And just as they were about to roll the stone over the tomb, while weeping and wailing, Mary and Martha checked one last time, looking out over the road to Bethany. But still, no Jesus.

This is exactly where you and I live.

When your life takes a sudden turn in the wrong direction, you pray your best, most passionate prayer. You pray and pray and pray some more. But still, no Jesus. Your finances are sinking, your marriage is struggling, your family is falling apart, your kids have gone astray, your health is deteriorating. You get down on your knees and you pray, fully believing that Jesus, the all-powerful, all-loving Savior will appear at any time and make things right. But still, no Jesus.

Every Christ follower knows what this is like. As my mother lay dying, I remember sitting by the hospital bed, looking over the spiritual horizon, waiting for Jesus to show up. Wrestling with his delay, I began to reason with him. *Why God? I mean, this is a good person! The world is bad enough as it is! My mom needs to stay on the planet!* Hour after hour, prayer after prayer, pleading after pleading, "standing out on the road to Bethany," waiting. But still, no Jesus. At least, nothing happening that I could see.

THE HEALER COMES

When Jesus finally arrived in Bethany, he was greeted by two different people who asked the same question. However, Jesus gave two separate and distinct answers. His answers do not conflict but, instead, were tailored to meet the specific need of each individual. Martha was the first to meet Jesus on the road. "'Lord,' Martha said to Jesus, 'if you had been here, my brother would not have died" (v. 21). Martha's meaning is plain: "Lord, why did you not come?" (Why would an all-powerful, all-loving God not show up?)

"Jesus said to her, 'Your brother will rise again.'

"Martha answered, 'I know he will rise again in the resurrection at the last day.'

"Jesus said to her, 'I am the resurrection and the life. The one who believes in me will live, even though they die; and whoever lives by believing in me will never die. Do you believe this?'" (vv. 23-26).

Make no mistake; Martha was searching for truth. She was having trouble harmonizing Jesus' power and love with his actions. Notice Jesus' response. If it was truth Martha was searching for, Jesus brought it. His response says, "Wait a minute, Martha. Who am I? Take a good look now. Your family knows the truth of my identity perhaps better than any of my other disciples. Who am I, Martha? Think about what's true . . . and about what this implies. Now, Martha, tell me, do you need to wait until the final resurrection for Lazarus to come out of that grave, or can I do it right now?"

Martha was looking for truth, and Jesus gave it to her. The truth Jesus dispensed resonated with her. This was the care and comfort for which she had been waiting, so she left the scene to search for Mary.

When Mary found Jesus she repeated her sister's words. John 11:32 says, "When Mary reached the place where Jesus was and saw him, she fell at his feet and said, 'Lord, if you had been here, my brother would not have died.'" Same meaning: "Where were you? Why didn't you come?" Different answer. This time Jesus responded not with a list of facts but with emotional tears[3]: "When Jesus saw her weeping, and the Jews who had come along with her also weeping, he was deeply moved in spirit and troubled. 'Where have you laid him?' he asked.

"'Come and see, Lord,' they replied" (vv. 33, 34).

And then, the shortest verse in the Bible, John 11:35: "Jesus wept." He shed tears. We tend to assume that Jesus lived his life on an even keel, and many portrayals of him convey a sort of perpetual serenity. But the Scripture contradicts such interpretation.

If Jesus' delay during Lazarus's sickness was confusing, his emotion at Lazarus's tomb might have been downright mesmerizing. After all, Jesus knew that in a few seconds he was going to bring Lazarus back to life! If I were Jesus and possessed that kind of power, I'd probably say, "Have no fear, Jesus is here!" or "Hold on to the women and children, stand back, and watch the power of God!" Instead, Jesus moved in close to Mary, sensed her pain, and began to weep.

> He just wept with her and, without saying a word, reminded her that he cared.

This scene, more than any other scene in the Bible, reminds me that we need both truth and tears when we are hurting. One without the other is almost offensive. Moreover, our personality types dictate when each should be given. So when Jesus met Martha, he said, "Hey, Martha, who am I? Remember? I have power over life and death. I am God and I can do all things." But when he met Mary, there were no truth statements or deductive reasoning. He just wept with her and, without saying a word, reminded her that he cared. Jesus always cares. That's a fact—and a promise we can depend on.

REALITY CHECK

As we get older, somewhere along the line it dawns on us: the Savior for whom our souls long is not just one of truth but also one of tears. And we *want* a Savior who truly cares.

When my mom died, many of my friends came to the funeral. Some gave me truth: "Jeff, remember, your mom's not in that casket. Your mom's not in the grave. She's with God, and she doesn't want to return." I appreciated such truth; but at the same time, I didn't need it. I wasn't doubting my mother's location. I knew that she was in Heaven and that she was happy. My sadness was the result of knowing that I wasn't going to see her for a very long time. Yes, truth was encouraging but still insufficient in dealing with the loss of someone who could never be replaced. Thank God, some of my friends also brought me tears. One such friend was Terry Barker.

Terry was the shooting guard on my high school basketball team. He was a true leader and encourager. Because I was the tallest player on the team, my high school basketball coach expected me to take control of the defensive rebounding. "No second shots, Vines!" he would yell. Or "Be a man and do your job!"

> Only Jesus is God and is able to see your circumstances from all angles. He alone knows what is really happening and the reason it is occurring.

Seconds before tip-off, seeing the overwhelming and often impossible tasks I had been given by the coach, Terry would come up to me, pat me on the backside, and whisper in my ear, "You can do it, big 'un!" He'd say, "I believe in you! You can do this!" While what he said was important, the manner in which he said it revealed that he understood the vastness of the task and truly empathized with my plight. His eyes and demeanor clearly communicated that he cared. And to be honest, many of my best performances can be traced back to his willingness to personally identify with my circumstances. But his greatest contribution to my life did not come during a basketball game.

I was at the funeral home after my mom died, when Terry Barker walked in. I didn't recognize him at first because it had been twenty years since I had seen him. Both of us had more body but less hair. He made his way to the front of the reception line, and without any kind of small talk, grabbed my hand as if it were yesterday, leaned forward, and with the look of great care and concern I remembered—and a tear in his eye—he whispered into my ear, "I believe in you, big 'un. You can do this."

Both truth and care had come at a time when I was facing the most difficult challenge of my life. Both truth and care were needed; both were provided.

What is the point? We need both truth and tears. Only Jesus can *perfectly* give both. Only Jesus is God and is able to see your circumstances from all angles. He alone knows what is really happening and the reason it is occurring. He alone knows the truth about what the Father is asking you to endure. And as for the tears, Jesus is able to empathize with you because this is the one and only God who humbled himself and became a man. Hebrews 2:17 says, "For this reason he had to be made like them, fully human in every way, in order that he might become a merciful and faithful high priest in service to God, and that he might make atonement for the sins of the people." He has experienced what you have experienced, and more. We should strive to be like him, and give others both truth and tears, though we will never give both perfectly as he does.

This is why the incarnation is so brilliant! When I hear someone say, "Jesus came to the earth to discover what it was like to be human," I say, "No! He's God! He already knows everything. Omniscience doesn't learn! He did not come to earth to discover information but to remove any doubt from *our* minds that he fully and truly understands our predicament. And he reminds us that life's tragedies do not mean that God has abandoned us; in fact, it is possible that in the midst of our deepest tragedies, we can be closer to God than at any other time (or as some might put it, we are never more in the center of God's will). God knows the truth about our circumstances, but he understands that truth is simply not enough. We need both truth and tears. We need to know God cares. We need to know he empathizes.

FIXERS VS. **FEELERS**

When it comes to the manner in which each of us relates to people who are hurting, some of us are fixers. We want to fix everything, and we want to fix it now. Somebody comes to us and says, "You know, I'm really having a hard time." So what do we do? We start spouting off Bible verses, one after the next, and we say, "You know, here are the three things wrong with you, and I'll give you six ways to fix your issues." Well, some people don't want to hear that! They don't need truth right now. They need love and empathy.

Others of us are feelers. We want to sympathize and cry with everybody, but we often are very uncomfortable confronting the sin that may be the primary cause of the pain. Feelers sometimes don't want to give anybody truth; they just want to say, "It's OK. Let's cry together. Let's invite all our friends over for a pity party." The feeler approach is good for a season, but only for a season. Sooner or later, truth needs to be injected into the situation. Feelers would never say, "Dude, you're crying because you made a mess of this. Repent! Let's go a different direction! OK?" This kind of language is just too hard for them.

I recall hearing author Tim Keller say that if you are a fixer only, you're not like Jesus; and if you are a feeler only, you're not like Jesus either. When the Spirit of God comes to live in us, he begins to shape and mold us into both feelers and fixers. This divine transformation gives us the ability to appropriate the right response at the right time. You recognize that there are Marthas and Marys in the world. When you meet the Marthas, those critical thinkers who live and die on professing the truths of God, you will present truth first, feelings later. However, when you meet the Marys of the world, the tenderhearted, emotion-driven temperaments, you will give feelings first—a soft touch or whisper, an affectionate hug or tender kiss—and truth later.

It is here that we begin to see how a God who allows tragedies in our lives also cares for us in the midst of them. Those who have been gifted with God's Spirit make up what is known as the church—a community of thinkers and feelers who love and support one another during difficult times. This is the hallmark of God's people. They love one another. They care for one another. Each person becomes a conduit of God's love, mercy, and compassion. We become the hands and feet of Jesus, as it is no longer we who live but Christ who lives in us (Galatians 2:20).

A CONTEMPORARY **EXAMPLE**

In 1982, Harvard's graduating seniors requested Mother Teresa as their commencement speaker.[4] This old Albanian woman dressed in white humbly strolled onto the platform and spoke on the topic of abstinence! Evidently, behind those soft eyes and compassionate demeanor was a warrior's heart. Abstinence at Harvard? Man, that's brave! The Harvard students booed her. Wow! How could you possibly boo Mother Teresa?

Meanwhile, some of the children Mother Teresa had rescued from the streets of Calcutta, India, were in the Boston area and had come to the graduation to surprise her. Hiding behind the columns, the children waited for their moment of opportunity. When the booing began, the children mistakenly assumed the speech was over and rushed the stage toward Mother Teresa. Suddenly, everything changed. The Harvard students, witnessing firsthand the powerful love and compassion with which this nun embraced her children, rose to their feet and offered a standing ovation. What changed? She had spoken the truth and been booed before. But when the crowd saw her love in action, they responded with respect.

The lesson about what people *see* is an important lesson to be learned. The church exists to spread the gospel, but if the church as a body does not invest in its surrounding community and care for it—that is, does not do things that are seen—no one will be able to *hear* the truth of the gospel message. Hearers of the message may not easily grasp the love that's behind it. The apostle Paul said, "If I . . . do not have love, I am only a resounding gong or a clanging cymbal" (1 Corinthians 13:1). If I am perceived that way, I might get booed right off the stage!

As a pastor I have heard hundreds of people claim that they don't need community. But the price of living and operating outside of community is too high. The church was designed by God to act as a community itself and to reach out to the community beyond. We believers benefit from the church community, of course, during times of loneliness, crisis, and tragedy, when everyone gathers around with love, help, and care. But we sometimes forget the extended responsibility of the church community: that God's presence is often felt through the love, mercy, and compassion of those inside whom the Spirit of God dwells. People need to see God's care through our care.

> We become the hands and feet of Jesus, as it is no longer we who live but Christ who lives in us.

Does God care? You bet your life he does. The incarnation (God lived in the world as a man) and the divine indwelling (the Holy Spirit lives in believers) demonstrate the lengths to which God will go to ensure our peace in the midst of some of the most tragic storms.

HEAD LEADS **THE HEART**

Among the college crowd at our church, I often hear such statements as, "Theology doesn't really matter. It's what's in here (*pointing to the heart*) that matters." Or "Faith is not a matter of the head but the heart." This kind of thinking is not only potentially dangerous but is also counterproductive. After all, the heart responds only to what the head believes. If we cry, it is because our head has told us that we ought to be sad. Hitler created a generation of young men who were able to kill without emotion. In other words, when a young soldier pulled the trigger and shot entire Jewish families at point-blank range, he was able to do so without hesitation because his head had been trained to think of Jewish people as nothing more than animals needing to become extinct.

The bottom line is that what we believe impacts what we feel and what we do. Consequently, our ability to connect with God and to endure the tragedies is directly related to what we believe about his workings and doings—in our lives directly or through the community that surrounds us.

BACK TO **THE STORY**

What on earth was Jesus doing in the lives of Mary, Martha, and Lazarus?

John 11:38 says, "Jesus, once more deeply moved, came to the tomb." Theologians are in a quandary over the interpretation of this passage. What does it mean to be *deeply moved*? The Greek word (also used in v. 33) "means literally 'to snort like a horse' and generally connotes anger."[5] If you want a word picture, think of a bullfighter waving the red cloak. What does the bull typically do? He snorts, bellows, and drags his hind leg, preparing to charge the fighter. Hard to imagine Jesus sporting a similar demeanor. Anger? Really? What exactly is Jesus charging? At what or whom was he angry as he approached the tomb?

> How do you scare a guy who's "been there, done that" where death is concerned?

I agree with the writer of *The Expositor's Bible Commentary,* that perhaps Jesus was expressing "his resentment against the ravages of death that had entered the human world because of sin."[6] I think he was calling sin and death out! It was showdown time at the Bethany Corral. Death was firing back: "You touch me, Jesus, and I'll touch you. You interrupt this funeral, and I'll cause yours."

Did you know that the raising of Lazarus was the beginning of the end for Jesus? Interesting, isn't it? Rather than believing in Jesus after this amazing miracle, the religious leaders began to plot how they might put him to death (v. 53).

Jesus was well aware that when he interrupted this funeral, it would hasten his own. He was more than willing to face his own death with courage and inner peace because he knew that he had come into the world for this very purpose. He knew that while facing the most tragic and horrible death possible, he would be in the very center of God's will. That is the truth of the matter.

He had come with truth to Martha, and he had shared tears with Mary. He knows and he cares. And when tragedy comes into my life and yours, we can have absolute certainty that Jesus knows what's going on and that he weeps with us. He has also provided us with his presence and a loving community that will escort us through the most painful experiences of our lives.

So Jesus moved toward the tomb of Lazarus with both truth and tears.

Not often do I adore the language of the *King James Version,* but here I thoroughly enjoy it. After instructing the crowd to remove the stone, Martha, the critical thinker, said, "Lord, by this time he stinketh: for he hath been dead four days" (v. 39, *KJV*). The body stinketh? I love that. "Then Jesus said, 'Did I not tell you that if you believe, you will see the glory of God?'" (v. 40). According to the rest of the text, Jesus prayed to the Father to ensure that the crowd understood the origin of the power about to be unleashed. Then Jesus called for Lazarus to come out of the tomb.

At that point the scene must have resembled a tennis match. The crowd looked at Jesus—then at the tomb—then to Jesus—then at the tomb—then to Jesus . . . well, you get the point. They had to be thinking, *Is this really going to happen? Is this even possible?* And then . . . the earth shook, a collective gasp erupted from the crowd, and Lazarus came out!

"Jesus said to them, 'Take off the grave clothes and let him go'" (v. 44). Do you think people were in a hurry to go up to this guy? No! They had to be a little freaked out here. They were probably all in shock!

"Uh . . . you go."

"*I'm* not going. You go."

"No way, man! I'm not going near that thing."

I wish the narrative continued. What did Lazarus say? How did this miracle change the rest of his life in Bethany? Better yet, was he ever afraid of anything again? How do you scare a guy who's "been there, done that" where death is concerned?

In a play entitled *Lazarus Laughed,* Eugene O'Neill puts words into the mouth of the resurrected Lazarus. The Roman leader Caligula is threatening him with . . . death! The situation strikes Lazarus as humorous, and he goes into gales of laughter. He finally catches his breath and says, "Caligula, haven't you heard? Death is dead!"[7]

Indeed, death *is* dead. And the power that killed death is what those of us who are hurting desire most. So when we pray and pray and still there's no Jesus, we begin to wonder whether perhaps God does not care, or that maybe we have become torn from his moorings. Why would an all-powerful, all-loving God who is able to stop suffering allow so much pain into my life?

The answer is found in three verses in the story:

- "When he heard this, Jesus said, 'This sickness will not end in death. No, it is for God's glory so that God's Son may be glorified through it'" (John 11:4).
- "Then Jesus said, 'Did I not tell you that if you believe, you will see the glory of God?'" (v. 40).
- "Many of the Jews who had come to visit Mary, and had seen what Jesus did, believed in him" (v. 45).

What is the common thread running through Jesus' responses to our question about why? God's glory. You may say, "Wait a minute! Are you telling me that Jesus loved Mary, Martha, and Lazarus and that they were very close friends but he allowed their pain and suffering so that his Father would be glorified?"

Unequivocally, yes! This is going to be very difficult to embrace until you have truly given everything to God in response to God's giving everything to you. Yes, God will care for us during the storms of our lives, but he still expects us to ride through the storms if it means that, in the process, he will be glorified and others will come to believe. That's how his kingdom is expanded. That is the lesson to be learned. Just as God's number-one priority for his own Son was not convenience, neither is it his number-one priority for us.

> When you believe that God is always in control of your circumstances and that no event has ever caught God by surprise, you will begin to exhibit a tranquility that will amaze those around you.

Conformity to Christ rather than *convenience* in this life is his number-one priority for all those who call on the name of the Lord Jesus. As we become more and more like Jesus, we are positioned to glorify God in a way that a life void of trouble never could. In fact, the authenticity of your faith is never more revealed or exposed than in times of pain and suffering. During these seasons of life we become walking, living, breathing testimonies to the power and care of God. He promises, "Cast your cares on the LORD and he will sustain you; he will never let the righteous be shaken" (Psalm 55:22). We must remember that the Spirit of him who raised Jesus from the dead lives in us today (Romans 8:11).

But make no mistake—your response to life's tragedies will be determined by your reason for living. This is the point at which the head impacts the heart, and you begin to feel and experience the primary means by which God cares for us during difficult times.

When you believe that God is always in control of your circumstances and that no event has ever caught God by surprise, you will begin to exhibit a tranquility that will amaze those around you. This is "the peace of God, which transcends all understanding" that the apostle Paul speaks of in Philippians 4:7. It comes when a person has made up his mind to live for a purpose greater than himself and feels great happiness knowing that God works all circumstances together for his good.

This is exactly what happened when the religious leaders of Paul's day persistently threatened the disciples if they didn't stop preaching the gospel. The disciples' response was, "We must obey God rather than human beings!" (Acts 5:29). As a result of their obeying God, the disciples were severaly beaten. "Then [the leaders] ordered them not so speak in the name of Jesus" (v. 40). Again. Yet after this horrible experience, how did the disciples respond?

"The apostles left the Sanhedrin, rejoicing because they had been counted worthy of suffering disgrace for the Name. Day after day, in the temple courts and from house to house, they never stopped teaching and proclaiming the good news that Jesus is the Messiah" (vv. 41, 42).

When you live for a purpose greater than yourself, the heart rejoices even in—or maybe *especially* in—times of suffering, because the head believes that such occasions bring glory to God and expand the kingdom of Christ.

A SHINING **EXAMPLE**

Greg Laurie is the senior pastor of a twenty-thousand-plus member church in Riverside, California. A dynamic speaker, Greg has often been referred to as the next Billy Graham. His Harvest Crusades draw thousands of people each year into stadiums around the country.

Greg's story is an amazing one. His path to becoming senior pastor of a megachurch was anything but typical, but he has stayed the course and weathered the storms in a way that has honored God for the last thirty-five years. In July 2008, Greg faced what he later described as his toughest test.[8] In a horrible car accident, his precious son Christopher was lost. The accident happened just weeks before Greg was scheduled to host the Southern California Harvest Crusade in the Los Angeles area.

People wondered whether he would go through with the crusade. Others were concerned about the impact that the accident and loss of a son would have on Greg's faith. Still others questioned God on Greg's behalf, demanding that God give an explanation for allowing such a faithful servant to experience such tragedy. Where on earth was God during this event? Where was God's care for a treasured son?

Greg, however, saw things from a different perspective. I later spoke with people who attended this event and described what happened. Greg Laurie stood up in the stadium, as scheduled, to preach to a crowd of more than 109,000 who were anxious to see how Greg would deal with the type of tragedy every parent fears most! Greg Laurie assured his audience that his faith was still intact and that, although there are thousands of things he does not understand about God, those hidden things do not change the hundreds of things he *does* understand—that God is good; and God is perfect; and God is sovereign; and if he allows a tragedy in our lives, such tragedies become strategic to his plan and goodwill.

At the close of Greg's message, 11,278 people flooded the infield to submit to the lordship of Jesus Christ. Eleven thousand! Even the press could not deny the reality of what happened on that field.

Young people had driven from all over the U.S.—the same young men and women that many people had given up on. The same college and university students who many claim are unreachable and uninterested in the things of God. Those who came were interviewed by the secular media in an attempt to discover why so many people had come to this particular 2008 Harvest Crusade. "Why now?"

The response was the same over and over and over again. They basically said, "I just wanted to know if Greg Laurie really believes what he says he believes, and when I found out that he did, I thought, *He's real. Therefore, Jesus is real. I'm going down on that infield!*"

The response to Greg's simple presentation of the gospel was so overwhelming that Los Angeles planned to host a second event in 2011, expecting to draw thousands more from all over the country. (The event occurred September 2011 and attracted fifty thousand people.)

Our young people have not given up on God; they have just given up on faith that is not authentic. Words do not mean as much to them as actions, and Greg's actions during an undeniably tragic event compelled them to take Jesus seriously. Like it or not, there is something hardwired into each of us that is moved and intrigued when someone responds to pain in the way Greg Laurie did. Suddenly our eyes are opened, our perspectives are changed, and we are drawn to the Savior who has the power to sustain us through the most tragic of circumstances.

OH YES, **HE CARES**

Does God care? Absolutely.

First, he expresses that care by giving us both truth and tears. Truth comes when we recognize that despite the appearance of God's abandonment, he is not only present; he is large and in charge! God is sovereign and is never caught by surprise. When tragedies come, he is in full control and often allows these unfortunate events for the purpose of expanding his kingdom on this earth. When hard times come to the person who has truly surrendered to Jesus at the cross, there's a greater chance of that person running *to* God rather than fighting him and running *from* him. The church joins the person in truth and tears, and those who don't know God see it all and have an opportunity to believe.

> Young people had driven from all over the U.S.—the same young men and women that many people had given up on.

Second, for those who have given it all to God, the Spirit of God reminds them that God is not a God who makes a sovereign decision and then stands back and says, "OK, this is what I have decided. Now deal with it!" Instead, God unleashes the church, his built-in mechanism to care for and comfort those who are hurting. God's new community in the world has been called to bear one another's burdens (Galatians 6:2) and to weep with those who weep, sorrow with those who sorrow, and rejoice with those who rejoice (see Romans 12:15). When the church does this well, the world sees a movement of people who consider it pure joy when trials come. The believers know that such trials enhance the power of Christ in their own lives, serve as a testimony to the world, and advance the kingdom of Christ.

What, then, shall we say in response to these things? If God is for us, who can be against us? He who did not spare his own Son, but gave him up for us all—how will he not also, along with him, graciously give us all things? . . . Who shall separate us from the love of Christ? Shall trouble or hardship or persecution or famine or nakedness or danger or sword? . . . No, in all these things we are more than conquerors through him who loved us. For I am convinced that neither death nor life, neither angels nor demons, neither the present nor the future, nor any powers, neither height nor depth, nor anything else in all creation, will be able to separate us from the love of God that is in Christ Jesus our Lord (Romans 8:31, 32, 35, 37-39).

God cares for you. He promises that no trouble or hardship will come your way that can separate you from his love. And that's the truth.

GREAT AND PRECIOUS PROMISES

For Christians, sacrifice means willingly surrendering ourselves to the will of God. And we don't do this because of what we will gain or even just because we know it is right. We do it out of gratitude for what God has already done for us through Jesus Christ, trusting that he will care for our every need. This living sacrifice involves the body, mind, and will. There can be no holding back. When we do this, God is glorified.

1 Have you ever had a "but still, no Jesus" moment? What happened?

2 Think back to a situation you have faced (or are currently facing right now) that made you question whether or not God cares. Why did the situation make you question God's love for you?

3 In the story of Lazarus's death, do you identify more with the needs of Martha or of Mary? Explain. Are you more a fixer or a feeler? What are some specific ways you could practice both fixing and feeling when another person is suffering?

4 Read Romans 12:1, 2 slowly. What hits you the most about this passage? If we are to be a living sacrifice to God, we have to trust that he will care for us and see us through even the darkest of days. What is keeping you from living as a sacrifice and trusting that God cares for you?

5 What does it mean to let God change the way you think (Romans 12:2)? How does the story of Jesus raising Lazarus from the dead impact your head and your heart about how God cares for us? How can the way you view what happens to you affect the way you worship and glorify God?

6 What keeps people from giving their bodies, their minds, and their wills to God for his service? Why is it so difficult for people to give those kinds of sacrifices?

CHAPTER THREE

I WILL.
GIVE YOU WHAT YOU NEED
MARK 2:1-12

AM I THE ONLY man on the planet who cried like a little baby at the end of *Toy Story 3*? Andy clutched his toys Woody and Buzz, trying to decide whether or not his two favorite childhood companions should remain in the family home or be taken with him to college. When he left them behind, I am not sure what came over me . . .

Sitting in the movie theater with my wife, I started thinking about my daughter, Sian, and my son, Delaney, soon going out into the great big world and leaving all their toys and their rooms behind. I just started crying! Then I had to lie to my wife when she asked, "Are you crying?"

I said, "No man, I'm not crying. I've got a cold!" *Big boys don't cry. A lesser man might cry, but not me!*

There is a common cord running throughout the Toy Story series, beyond the unique relationship between Andy and his toys. It's a theme of friendship, primarily between Buzz and Woody. They help the other toys, as well as each other, discover meaning and significance. Making Andy happy is the ultimate goal, and every toy wants to know that it plays a crucial and important role in making that happen.

Toy Story world is a kind of microcosm of the world outside Andy's room, *our* world. Meaning and significance drive much of what we say and do. Much of the non-toy, human world spends its time chasing the elusive dream, assuming that if we could just grab hold of that one thing, then we would be happy, fulfilled . . . and all would be well for the rest of our lives! Such is the backdrop against which we read the narrative of Mark 2.

In this second chapter of Mark's Gospel, we meet a man desperately longing for healing. You must put yourself in his position: he was a paralyzed man who lived on a mat that I think we can assume was about six feet long by four feet wide. Imagine living your entire life within those confines. He was not mobile. He was restricted to the parameters of the mat, and without the assistance of others, his horizons would never be expanded.

Somebody else had to feed, carry, change, and clothe this guy. Worse yet, no medical hope existed. No hospitals, surgeries, rehabilitation facilities, or treatment centers were available. Yet he probably still dreamed about what it would be like to walk or to run or to have a family of his own . . . or even a place of business where he would be respected by the local community. However, all those dreams were merely that: dreams. Without a miracle, he had no hope of anything ever changing.

The narrative tells us that the man was totally dependent on the kindness and compassion of four friends.

MY FRIEND **ANDREW**

Andrew was a very good friend of mine in high school. Handsomely built and possessing admirable athletic prowess, Andrew was the envy of most guys. Unfortunately, Andrew was a little (OK, a lot) on the wild side, especially when he was behind the wheel of a car. I was astounded when Andrew's parents gave him a brand-new Pontiac Trans-Am for his sixteenth birthday. I had no doubt that this was an accident waiting—if not begging—to happen. Not surprisingly, within a matter of weeks, Andrew totaled his car in an accident that left him paralyzed from the waist down.

> What he really needed was a Savior to lift him up and out of temporal pursuits and propel him toward a life that transcends the self and goes hard after eternal things.

Not deterred in any way, Andrew's parents purchased another car that could be operated solely from the steering column. Andrew was still able to race his car at dangerous speeds; and within a few more months . . . another wreck, another tragedy, another sad situation. This time the paralysis was from the neck down.

Over the years I visited Andrew on numerous occasions. Each time I wondered how a young man, full of passion and life, could survive the confines of a hospital bed and the four walls within which he would spend much of the rest of his life. I watched as Andrew desperately attempted to live above his circumstances. He tried to attach himself to things that would somehow bring meaning to his life. At first it was the Elizabethton Twins, our hometown minor league baseball team. As long as they were winning, Andrew's spirits were high, hope abounding. However, if the Twins started losing, he would fall into times of deep depression.

After the Twins it was the East Tennessee State Buccaneers, our NCAA Division I college basketball team. Again, as long as they were winning, Andrew was up! But if they were losing, he seemed to feel that his life was worthless and insignificant. What he really needed was a Savior to lift him up and out of temporal pursuits and propel him toward a life that transcends the self and goes hard after eternal things.

A sports team could never live up to that expectation. By the age of thirty-five, Andrew's roller-coaster ride had finally gotten to him. With the assistance of someone else, Andrew committed suicide.

While there are similarities between Andrew's story and that of the disabled man in Mark 2, one distinction is crystal clear. This guy had four friends who were willing to do whatever it took to change his world. And in this case, "whatever it took" meant getting him to Jesus.

AMAZING **FRIENDS**

Those four friends were amazing indeed! In the ancient world many people, for various reasons, behaved callously toward those who were disabled. In some circles, if parents gave birth to a defective infant, they were instructed to drown the child in the river. A Roman code of law from 500 BC read: "Kill quickly . . . a dreadfully deformed child."[1] Aristotle wrote, "With regard to the choice between abandoning an infant or rearing it, let there be a law that no crippled child be reared."[2]

In ancient Judaism, as indicated in certain documents, there was the view that all life is a blessing, regardless.[3] At least on paper. Yet even in the religious world of Israel, if your child was born with some kind of deformity, it seemed to be commonly assumed that you were the worst of sinners and were on the receiving end of God's wrath. Note the question of Jesus' disciples, regarding the man born blind: "Who sinned, this man or his parents, that he was born blind?" (John 9:2).

So often through history there has been a stigma concerning physical deformities or mental illness. Yet the four friends in Mark 2 were of a different mind-set. They made huge sacrifices for their friend.

Once you become friends with somebody on a mat, that person's problems become your problems. In this case, it was a matter of utter dependence.

If you want to know what utter dependence looks like, talk to a mother with young children. Ask her to explain the difference between life BC (before children) and AC (after children). She might describe how before children, she used to go to the beach, relax, soak up the sun rays, listen to the roar of the ocean waves, and fall asleep in the shade. After children is a different story. Now she has to keep an eye on the children, making sure they don't drown in the ocean, eat sand, or get kidnapped by some stranger! It's a relationship of utter dependence.

The four friends did not run from their friend's utter dependence, and that's what made them so special! When they heard that Jesus was in town, they started to dream of the possibilities: *What if we could get our friend to Jesus? Jesus could heal him!*

They must have realized that getting their paralyzed friend to Jesus was going to be a logistical nightmare. Jesus was like a rock star! Thousands and thousands of people wanted to see him. They would have to elbow their way through the masses and break through the barriers. That would be difficult enough for one person just walking in. Throw in three other guys carrying a man on a mat, and it would seem impossible! But the four friends would not be deterred. They knew what their friend needed, and they were willing to do whatever it took.

SRO

The Bible says that when they arrived at the house where Jesus was speaking, it was SRO—standing room only. It was the first century, so there wasn't much else to do in town. No *Oprah,* no *CSI: Las Vegas,* no *CSI: Miami,* no *CSI: NY,* No *CSI: Los Angeles* (I know there is no *CSI: Los Angeles,* but just wait—there will be), no health clubs, and no movie theaters. So when Jesus came to town, the crowds just flooded in. There was no room inside the house, and there was no room outside either. People everywhere—sitting and standing on the inside, listening and watching from the outside. Imagine how frustrated the four friends felt. So close and yet so far.

One of the four friends must have been an out-of-the-box thinker. Can't you hear him saying, "Hey, guys! What if we climb to the top of the house, dig a hole in the roof, and lower him right down in front of Jesus?"

Vandalism seemed to be the best approach! But it really wasn't vandalism. Most first-century houses featured stairs on the outside that led to a type of roof patio. The roof was generally made of wooden beams covered with branches and packed with clay.[4] So subtle changes in these roofs were easily repaired. Perhaps because no one could come up with a better idea, these four guys climbed to the top and began to dig!

> **They knew what their friend needed, and they were willing to do whatever it took.**

Think about what you would have seen from the inside. At first you'd just see eight hands rooting around up above—that had to be weird—kind of clearing the branches, and twigs and clay would be falling down on Jesus' head while he was trying to teach. Everyone must have been looking at Jesus, glancing upward, then back at Jesus . . . anticipating his response. Maybe such an interruption was a rare event. It was the first century, when preachers were not interrupted by cell phones, pagers, beepers, and other gadgets from the underworld. Yet here were four friends, convinced that if they could just get their friend to Jesus, Jesus would give him what he needed.

Now who do you think was most impressed by the rude interruption? Jesus. Mark 2:5 states, "When Jesus saw *their* faith, he said to the paralyzed man, 'Son, your sins are forgiven'" (emphasis added). Wow! Do you know what this means? The faith of four friends brought salvation to another.

WHO ARE **YOU CARRYING?**

Before we move on I have to ask, who's on the mat that you are carrying? Surely there is someone, and you know it's going to take great sacrifice; it's going to be incredibly inconvenient. But you don't care. You are willing to do whatever it takes. Surely if you've been saved by the grace of God and you're passionate about your faith, there is at least one person on a mat you are hauling around.

Someone you are desperately trying to get to Jesus, firmly believing that Jesus will give the person what he or she truly needs.

Not too long ago, Michael, a member of our church here in Southern California, introduced us to his new friend, a homeless man named Marvin. Michael's small group had adopted Marvin and had begun to "carry his mat." They looked after his social needs, gave him some clothes, provided food and shelter, and invested in his life. As a result, Marvin was drawn to our church and to our Savior. He is now attending church every week, trusting Jesus to give him what he truly needs. But what he needed to get there in the first place was some friends to carry his mat.

FORGIVEN **SINS**

Now why did the four friends bring the paralyzed man to Jesus? To heal him, right? Can you imagine those friends on the roof, looking down, thinking, *This is going to be great.* And then Jesus looked at the paralyzed man and said, "Son, your sins are forgiven" (Mark 2:5).

> Jesus often resists giving us something that brings only temporary satisfaction.

I can imagine the four friends up on the roof, looking at each other and asking, "What? Did he say what we think he said? Hey, Jesus, thanks, but that's not why we brought him to you! We'll take one healing to go, please." What on earth was Jesus doing?

Verse 6 shows that some of the religious leaders were present. Was Jesus merely trying to engage them in some theological discussion? Knowing what the self-righteous teachers of the law were thinking, Jesus beat them to the punch and asked, "Which is easier, to heal or to forgive sins?" (v. 9, my paraphrase).

Which *is* easier? Forgiving someone's sins seems to me to be the more difficult of the two. While the number of those who have possessed the gift of healing is quite small, only one person had ultimate power and authority to forgive sins. However, the one who has the power and authority to forgive sins would have little difficulty in healing any and all physical disease.

WHAT WE **REALLY NEED**

Here is what I believe was happening. While still being sympathetic to the paralyzed man's suffering, Jesus was reminding him—and his friends and all within hearing—that there was a deeper issue at stake. Jesus' message is relevant to everyone who believes that if they could just obtain that one earthly thing for which their heart ultimately longs, then life would be good. Jesus was challenging the paralyzed man to consider the shallowness of his longings. But is a desire for healing necessarily "shallow"?

Think about it for a moment. You and I often say things like, "God, if you just give me that job promotion, then my life will be complete." Or "God, if you will just get me out of debt and help me through this tough economy, then I will have everything I need and will be happy and content." Or "God, if you will make my son or daughter, husband or wife, healthy again, then I will never ask you for anything else."

Yet if and when God delivers the goods, it's not very long before we begin playing that same game again. Jesus addressed the disabled man in the way he did because he knows that discontentment runs deep in the human heart.

It may be difficult for us to comprehend, but the reality is that Jesus often resists giving us something that brings only temporary satisfaction. Rather than constantly giving us what we *think* we cannot live without, Jesus seems committed to giving us what we truly need. Yes, the Bible does say:

- God is aware of our need for food, shelter, and clothing (Matthew 6:31, 32).
- God is very much aware of all that we need (Matthew 6:7, 8).
- God is able to bless us beyond what we actually need (2 Corinthians 9:8).
- God will supply all our needs (Philippians 4:19).

But Jesus constantly warns us to keep these needs in perspective.

While there is nothing inherently wrong with desiring good health, adequate finances, wonderful relationships, or even grand success, we tend to believe the lie that such things will fulfill the deepest longings of our heart and soul. Jesus might provide health, wealth, relationships, or success. But what we *really* need is Jesus himself. Jesus might merely have healed the physical ailments of the paralyzed man in this Scripture, but healing of another kind was what the man really needed.

SEEKING WHAT WE *DON'T* REALLY NEED

Unfortunately, our world is littered with people who have tried or are trying to fill an eternal void with temporary things. Guy de Maupassant was an incredibly talented writer of short stories, who rose from obscurity to fame within ten years. Soon he was so wealthy that he had a yacht on the Mediterranean, a house on the Normandy coast, and a luxurious flat in Paris. One author described him this way: "Critics praised him, men admired him and women worshipped him."[5] Maupassant possessed what the masses believed would bring ultimate peace, happiness, and satisfaction.

Yet in 1892, at the height of his career, he tried to cut his own throat. Placed in an insane asylum on the French Riviera, Maupassant lived out the rest of his short life. He was forty-two years old and had written his own epitaph: "I have coveted everything and taken pleasure in nothing."[6]

Fascinating, isn't it? Placing one's hope in anything temporary is similar to what happens when bugs are drawn to the dreaded bug zapper. No matter how many bugs end up in the tray of carnage, other bugs don't catch on. They continue to be drawn by the shiny, blue light . . . and into death.

And for us humans who continue to be drawn to things we only think we need, the result can be devastating, debilitating, and even deadly.

When most people think of the movie *Chariots of Fire,* they think of Eric Liddell, the Scottish runner who treasured his relationship with Christ and remained unwilling to allow anything, even an Olympic medal, to take precedence over his commitment to his Savior. While I admire Liddell, my fascination lies with Harold Abrahams, Liddell's archrival. Before the race, Abrahams said, "I will raise my eyes and look down that corridor; 4 feet wide, with 10 lonely seconds to justify my whole existence. But WILL I? . . . I've known the fear of losing but now I am almost too frightened to win."[7]

Do you see what he's saying? Better to chase the elusive dream, latching on to the mere *possibility* of discovering the meaning and significance to life, than to catch the dream and realize that nothing has changed and the feelings of hopelessness, meaninglessness, and insignificance linger on.

Pause.

Think.

What is that one elusive dream that drives you? You keep saying to yourself, "Man, if I could just _____, then my life would be complete, fulfilled, and purposeful." Whatever that thing is, it has become your idol. It is that on which you have hung ultimate worth, and God becomes the means to an end.

Ironic, isn't it? We end up calling on God not to help us *get rid of* our idols but to help us *get* our idols! "God, please help me obtain this one thing that will bring ultimate happiness. Help me get this one thing that has taken your place in my life."

In the early days of my ministry in New Zealand, we attracted some rather famous actors, actresses, and athletes. Intrigued by their presence at our church one day, I invited a few of them over for a cup of coffee in an effort to discover the things about our church they found so compelling. Their responses went something like this:

- "I'm here because I believe God will enable me to achieve all my goals and objectives and wealth."
- "I think God will make me a better and smarter businessman so that I can close these accounts and gain more profit."
- "I need God in my corner because I have some big opportunities coming up, and I need to know he's on my side."

In the end, I had learned something: I had done a poor job communicating the gospel. True Christ followers are not consumed with the question: "How can Jesus help me get the things I want or the things I think I can't live without?" Authentic Christ followers ask, "What does Christ require of me that his kingdom might be expanded on this earth through my life?"

> "God, please help me obtain this one thing that will bring ultimate happiness. Help me get this one thing that has taken your place in my life."

Peter was asked to give up his very life so that Christ would be glorified (John 21:18, 19). This is a sacrifice some are called to make. Those of us who live in the affluent West may never be asked to give up our lives; however, we may be asked to give up some of the stuff that affluence brings. Let's face it: wealth brings more and more things that tempt us away from God. We are indeed distracted by affluence. This stifles God's work in our lives and forfeits our opportunity to be used by God for purposes greater than ourselves.

My experience with the celebrities reminded me that many of us have fallen into the bad habit of asking God to do *our* will, instead of asking for God's will to be done. We want to involve God in helping us acquire whatever it is we've decided has the most worth. But Jesus wants to get us to the point where we realize that everything we truly need is found in him. If we have Jesus, we have it all. This is why the apostle Paul says, "I consider everything a loss because of the surpassing worth of knowing Christ Jesus my Lord, for whose sake I have lost all things. I consider them garbage, that I may gain Christ" (Philippians 3:8).

Unfortunately, we can easily fall into the trap of believing that when God does not give us what we think we can't live without, this is a sure sign of his abandonment. The Bible paints an entirely different picture. A major objective of the Holy Spirit is to strip you of everything you depend on other than God so that God will be the only one left on whom you *can* depend.

Do you recall the story from Judges 7 of a reluctant leader named Gideon? Before God was willing to use Gideon to defeat the Midianites (a well-armed, well-trained people), he escorted Gideon through a long series of tests and processes designed to reduce his army of 32,000 down to 300 men. With this small army of 300 untrained farmers, Gideon, with no significant military means, squared off against 135,000 Midianites! (Judges 8:10). By the way, that's 450-to-1 odds.

> When God becomes everything to us, our desires and needs begin to conform to the heart of God and to his goals for our lives.

All they had were trumpets and clay-jar torches. Of course, they possessed a very special secret weapon: God! That's what they needed; otherwise, Israel might boast that their own strength had saved them. Gideon's story is an example of how God removes all the things in which we place our hope and trust so that he may be glorified and his kingdom may be expanded on the earth.

Let's face it. Most of what we think we need, we just don't need. And many of our desires are unquenchable! Our desire for money, for example, is built on the false view that it is possible to get enough money to feel satisfied. But we soon find that the "thirst" is not quenched. God, however, knows what will bring ultimate fulfillment. He knows what we truly need and is committed to bringing us to the point where our desires for ourselves are aligned with his desires for us (see Matthew 6:10). When God becomes everything to us, our desires and needs begin to conform to the heart of God and to his goals for our lives. For example, our desire for personal gain might be replaced by a desire to be generous to others. We gain full lives when we finally let our personal desires go.

A CHANGE **IN HEART**

I watched the movie *Narnia: Voyage of the Dawn Treader,* based on the book by C. S. Lewis. In this story, we met a young man by the name of Eustace. It was clear within the first fifteen minutes of the movie how selfish, envious, and bitter this little boy was. The ship on which Eustace was traveling anchored near an island, and Eustace began an exploration. Coming to a cave of gold, jewels, and priceless treasures, Eustace began plotting his revenge against those whom he considered his enemies. With such wealth, he would have the power to achieve that for which his heart most longed—retribution.

Exhausted from his successful exploration, Eustace fell asleep on some of the treasures. When he woke up the next day, he discovered that he had become a dragon!

To me it was the perfect analogy: all the corruption on the *inside* had visibly transformed his exterior. With this unfortunate transformation came alienation. He could not return to the ship, to his friends, or to his enemies. They would kill a dragon.

When Eustace had come to the point of giving up hope, he (in dragon form) met Aslan the lion (the Christ figure). I watched as Aslan led Eustace to a clean pool of water and suggested that he undress and jump on in. Eustace must have wondered, *How can I undress? Underneath this dragon, is it still me?* With great hope and anticipation, Eustace made vigorous attempts to peel off the dragon flesh, but to no avail.

Patiently, Aslan approached and asked to undress the boy. Eustace was obviously afraid of Aslan's claws, but there seemed to be no other choice. So Eustace submitted to the painful procedure, which, of course, worked . . . and Eustace became a boy again.

What's the point?

God has to take his "claws" and go deeper and deeper, all the way to your heart, before he can change the thoughts and desires that are wreaking havoc on your life. The process will not be easy, nor will it be painless, but it has to be done. When we come to the point of desiring something so much that we believe our ultimate happiness and fulfillment is based on its acquisition, then that thing has become our idol—and the work God must do to rid us of it is painful.

Unfortunately, many people go through their entire lives stretching and straining for their idols, interpreting the failure to obtain them as God's abandonment. In reality, God has never left them and is waiting for them to realize that he is all they really need. When one finally comes to this understanding—that is, when a person's total allegiance is for God and the ultimate motivation is for God's glory—it is amazing what God begins to do. When a person lets go of his idols, instead of losing his life he feels restored, renewed, and perhaps alive for the very first time.

THE REST OF **THE STORY**

I believe that when Jesus told the paralyzed man "Son, your sins are forgiven," he was reminding all of us that until we are right with God, we will never really feel alive nor will we take hold of what we desperately long for: meaning, purpose, and significance. Temporary things cannot satisfy our longings. Only God can meet our deepest needs.

> In reality, God has never left them and is waiting for them to realize that he is all they really need.

It's as if Jesus looked at the disabled man and said, "OK, I've taken care of the deeper issue. Now pick up that mat, stand up, and walk out of here!"

And he did!

Think about this: if the man had been paralyzed for a long time, his muscles would have atrophied. So Jesus not only restored the paralyzed tissue and nerves but also gave him muscle tone! The guy just walked out! His four friends would have scrambled down the side of the house, met him at the front door, and launched a party that would have raised the roof! (OK, bad analogy.) Yes, Jesus gave him what he *wanted,* but most importantly, he gave the disabled man what he really *needed.* Christ is committed to doing no less for you. It's a promise.

• "Do not worry about your life, what you will eat or drink; or about your body, what you will wear. . . . Look at the birds of the air; they do not sow or reap or store away in barns, and yet your heavenly Father feeds them. Are you not much more valuable than they?" (Matthew 6:25, 26).

- "The LORD will keep you from all harm—he will watch over your life; the LORD will watch over your coming and going both now and forevermore" (Psalm 121:7, 8).

NEEDS THAT ARE **NOT IDOLS**

Our longings do not always become idols. Sometimes the things with which we are most concerned do not evolve into idols but are simple, everyday struggles that make us yearn for God's deliverance:

- a child who is ill
- an emotional wound that grows deeper and deeper
- a lack of food, water, and shelter essential to survival

Those reflect real needs rather than unquenchable desires. When we hand those needs over completely to our sovereign God—who has proven to be faithful and trustworthy—we can trust that he knows what he's doing. He has promised to care for us in these ways (and more):

- teach us his ways (Psalm 32:8)
- give us his peace (John 14:27)
- grant us his deliverance (Psalm 72:12)
- give us his strength (Philippians 4:13)

GOD KEEPS **HIS PROMISE**

I do not have an answer for why God allows so much pain into some people's lives. What I do know is that whatever God calls us to endure, he assumes the responsibility to equip us to endure it (1 Corinthians 10:13; 2 Corinthians 12:9). God will give you exactly what you need in every circumstance, if you run to him.

But sometimes what you need is endurance, courage, or faith—not the absence of hunger or need. A greater purpose, an eternal one, is at stake. God may have orchestrated your season of scarcity for purposes greater than yourself. God's kingdom may be glorified through your times of want. Even

Paul said that he had learned to be content "in plenty or in want" (Philippians 4:12). There were seasons in Paul's life when, despite much prayer, his physical needs remained unmet. And yet he discovered contentment. In other words, God gave him what he truly needed—the strength to endure those times and the peace that would, even in the darkest moments, keep him from despair.

In some unseen way God will use our unmet need to glorify himself and expand his kingdom here on the earth. That's the real promise! God works everything together for good (Romans 8:28).

Martyred missionary Jim Elliot once said, "He is no fool who gives what he cannot keep to gain that which he cannot lose."[8] For the authentic follower of Jesus Christ, giving up what he cannot keep in order to gain what he cannot lose becomes commonplace. Life is the greatest need of all; yet some are asked to give it up. Though we all die, because of Christ we will live again; and the life we now have doesn't even compare with the life that shall be. God will ultimately give us all that we need. You can count on it!

My friend Ajai Lall lives in India and leads pastors who are turning the world "right side up" with the gospel. He brought me to tears as he described the faith and commitment of his young preachers. Each new day brings the threat of death: they are torched, beaten with iron rods, dipped in hydrochloric acid, raped, and tortured . . . on a daily basis! Yet their request to the American church is not for prayers that the persecution will end, but for prayers that these pastors will be brave and courageous enough to endure it—because that is how the kingdom grows. They are praying that God will give them what they need—courage.

God is granting their request. Those pastors are relentless in the face of danger. Why? Because they live for a purpose greater than themselves and truly believe that whatever they give up in this life, God will more than make up for in the next. The most important thing in the here and now is that the kingdom of God is expanded on the earth through their lives.

Perhaps Corrie Ten Boom said it better than anyone else. During their horrific experience in the concentration camps of the Third Reich, she and her sister learned: "There is no pit so deep that God's love is not deeper still."[9] Even in our darkest hour we must never despair. God says that he will always give us what we truly need. And that's a promise.

GREAT AND PRECIOUS PROMISES

FOR INDIVIDUAL OR GROUP STUDY

During Jesus' ministry, he chose to spend much of his time with the outcasts of society. He could often be seen conversing, dining, and questioning those who were viewed by the religious standards of his day to be "far from God." Jesus knew what others did not—first, that God loves all people, even those who are far from him; and second, God often uses his people to build relationships that will draw others close to him.

1 Reflect on your past for a moment. How did God meet a spiritual, emotional, financial, or relational need? What did you learn about God through that experience?

2 What genuine need presently exists in your life? An illness? Financial needs? Relational needs? Ask yourself, *What is God trying to teach me during this season of my life? How is he going to use this to give me what I really need?*

3 What "needs" (perhaps idols) are presently wreaking havoc in your life? What things have you placed too much value on? Ask God to open your eyes to misplaced trust. Ask him to forgive you and to give you the Holy Spirit's power to overcome the idols in your life.

4 Jesus did not say, "If you build it they will come." He said, "Go" (Matthew 28:18-20). Who have you gone to—to invest in that person's life, to carry him or her closer to Jesus? What are you willing to do in order to get that person closer to Jesus?

5 How are you living for a purpose greater than your own desires? Whose need is God calling you to meet? Whose need remains unmet because you have not yet responded to the call? It will require time, energy, and great effort. It may be inconvenient, painstaking, and downright bothersome at times, but it will also be Christlike. Are you in? What specific steps will you take this week to help meet the needs that you see before you?

CHAPTER FOUR

I WILL
SAVE YOU
JOHN 19:16-18, 29, 30; 20:24-31

T HE PROPHET JOEL SAID it (Joel 2:32), and more than eight hundred years later, the apostle Paul repeated it: "Everyone who calls on the name of the Lord will be saved" (Romans 10:13). Of all the enduring promises we find in Scripture, no other promise holds greater significance for both this life and the one to come.

But what does salvation really mean? From what is one saved? Why is salvation something we should be concerned about? Before God's promise of "I will save you" can become precious to us, we must understand the answers to those questions. That will require a bit of a journey.

WHAT REALLY HAPPENED **THE DAY JESUS DIED?**

John, one of Jesus' disciples, gives us a historical account of Jesus' crucifixion. Many Christians read through John 19 and 20 failing to consider the totality of all that is represented in John's account. For instance, we are told that "Pilate took Jesus and had him flogged" (John 19:1). Remember that Jesus was scourged (flogged) by Pilate after a night of anguish in an unlawful courtroom, which included hours of unquenched thirst and multiple beatings.

You may not be familiar with the scourging process. The third-century historian Eusebius, who was eyewitness to many crucifixions, described a scourging as a severe punishment during which "the sufferer's veins were laid bare, and the very muscles, sinews and bowels of the victim were open to exposure."[1]

The relentless torture meant that many men died before they ever made it to the cross. Thus, scourging was sometimes referred to as the halfway death, since it stopped just short of death.[2]

John 19:17 tells us that Jesus had to carry his own cross. Then the Romans would have stretched out his arms, driven five- to seven-inch-long spikes into his wrists near the median nerve, which would be crushed on impact. The pain of crucifixion was beyond severe. In fact, our word *excruciating* is from the verb *cruciare* ("to crucify," "to torment"), which is from *crux,* meaning "cross."[3]

Next, the nails would have been driven through Jesus' feet, once again crushing his nerves and shocking his body. The stress of hanging on a tree causes a slow, painful death. Seneca, a first-century Stoic, wrote: "Can anyone be found who would prefer wasting away in pain dying limb by limb, or letting out his life drop by drop, rather than expiring once for all? Can any man be found willing to be fastened to the accursed tree, long sickly, already deformed, swelling with ugly weals on shoulders and chest, and drawing the breath of life amid long drawn-out agony? He would have many excuses for dying even before mounting the cross."[4]

Today our forms of capital punishment may vary, but in almost all cases the circumstances are highly controlled. Death comes quickly and predictably, and medical examiners carefully certify the victim's passing. Comparatively, crucifixion is neither quick nor predictable.

Jesus willingly endured the cross for one reason: he wanted to save us. John recorded Jesus' final words: "It is finished" (19:30). But Jesus didn't stay dead. In three days he rose from the grave. So what was "finished" wasn't Jesus' life but the work of salvation.

Jesus went on to perform other signs and miracles after his resurrection. Why? "Jesus performed many other signs in the presence of his disciples, which are not recorded in this book. But these are written that you may believe that Jesus is the Messiah, the Son of God, and that by believing you may have life in his name" (20:30, 31).

Jesus was sent from God to accomplish the most important mission ever, a mission we can't accomplish on our own: our salvation. But sometimes we just can't see it.

OUR **ARROGANCE**

I read a series of articles about the ten most difficult things to do in the world of sports.[5] According to the author, number four on the list involved hitting a golf ball long and straight. As a low handicap golfer (4.2), I immediately began to feel superior to the rest of the human race. I had never tried pole vaulting—number three—nor had I driven a race car at high speeds—number two—but since I knew I was able to hit a golf ball long and straight, I thought to myself, *How difficult can those things really be?* Scanning the article with great anticipation, I moved forward to the number-one most difficult thing to do and quickly took a slice of humble pie when I read what it was: hitting a fastball at Major League speeds. Ouch!

Nails would have been driven through Jesus' feet, once again crushing his nerves and shocking his body.

Several years ago I had the opportunity to hit a fastball delivered from a Dodger great, Orel Hershiser. While living in New Zealand, my wife and I had taken a vacation to Australia's Gold Coast. One of the theme parks featured a batting cage where you could face the Major League pitcher of choice. I chose Hershiser. Suddenly, there he was on a huge projection screen, going into his windup with the crowd behind him and the infield taunting, "Hey batter, batter." Just as Hershiser completed his windup, a baseball traveling 88 miles per hour shot out of a hole in the screen. Before I could even think about swinging the bat, there was a loud noise just behind me. It was the sound of the rubber mat absorbing the baseball!

I dug in, hunkered down, and readied myself for the next delivery. Thirty minutes later I managed to foul-tip the ball. I was pumped! After a full hour, I finally parked a fastball deep over the left field and screamed, "Yeah! Did you see that! It's outta here! That baby is gone!"

Then a rather cynical twelve-year-old kid shouted, "Yes, but you turned the speed down to 44 miles per hour."

Every time I recall that experience, I think of the gap between what I *thought* I could do and what I actually could do. Talk about overestimating one's ability! This is precisely the situation on the television show *American Idol.* Most of the people who attend the tryouts have overestimated their ability and need to be told, "You can't sing! Don't go on *American Idol!* People are going to laugh at you!" I mean, seriously, where are their friends? A true friend would never let you embarrass yourself on national television, right? I would hope that my friends and family love me enough to tell me, "Dude, you can't sing. You need to try something else!"

In no area is there more of a gap between who we really are and who we think we are than in the area of righteousness. When it comes to "goodness," most of us are like those who try out for *American Idol*: we are just not that good. But in the area of goodness, instead of comparing ourselves with the likes of a Mother Teresa or a Billy Graham, we like to line ourselves up with the Charles Mansons of the world. After all, standing next to serial killers and cult leaders, we look pretty good!

The problem is that God is not like your high school biology teacher. He does not grade on a curve. Furthermore, entrance into Heaven is not earned by ensuring that the good outweighs the bad.

GOD DOES NOT GRADE **ON A CURVE**

We have this false sense of security that tells us that as long as we are at least 51 percent good, we will go to Heaven. I ask people all the time, "Are you going to Heaven?"

And they say yes.

But when I ask them why, their answer is usually something like, "Well, because I'm good" or "I'm not a bad person. I've never killed anybody, and I've never done any really bad things."

As soon as I hear this kind of argument, I immediately pull out a piece of paper and ask, "On a scale of one to ten, ten being the highest level of goodness and one being the lowest level of goodness, where would you write your name?" Without exception, the person always places himself somewhere just above the five. I have yet to meet one person who felt comfortable placing his or her name below the halfway mark. Why? Because most people assume that in order to get to Heaven, you have to be more good than bad.

> We have this false sense of security that tells us that as long as we are at least 51 percent good, we will go to Heaven.

At this point, I enjoy watching the tension increase as I tell them that when Mother Teresa was asked to rate herself on a similar graph, she wrote her name somewhere around the three-to-four level. As soon as I ask them whether or not they would now like to make an adjustment on the graph, they immediately grab the pen and write their name just underneath that mark. Continuing the conversation I usually inform them that Billy Graham was also asked the same question and wrote his name somewhere down around the two-to-three level. Again, the person usually cannot grab the pen fast enough to erase his name and rewrite it just *underneath* where Billy Graham wrote his.

Amazing, isn't it? The problem in our thinking stems from the false assumption that God somehow grades on a curve. The Bible teaches, however, that our standard is God—not any human being. And if we choose to relate to God on the basis of moral goodness, we will lose every time (Romans 3:20).

EPIC **FAILURE**

The Bible says, "All have sinned and fall short of the glory of God" (Romans 3:23). "There is no one righteous, not even one" (v. 10). Many have tried but all have failed. Jack Johnson wrote a song titled "Good People" that asks, "Where'd all the good people go?" According to the Bible, they were never here in the first place. Other than Jesus, there is no such thing as a "good person." Yes, when compared to other people, some people may be relatively good, but the Bible is clear: God is the standard, and compared to him no one is righteous. No matter how hard one tries to be good, there is always a measure of badness in all of us that continually drives a wedge between us and God.

J. I. Packer said, "Scripture shows that in God's estimate, some sins are worse and bring greater guilt than others, and that some sins do us more damage. Moses rates the golden calf debacle a great sin (Exodus 32:30). . . . John distinguishes sins that do and do not inevitably lead to death (1 John 5:16). . . . On one level, all sins are equal in that no matter how trivial they seem, they all deserve God's wrath. . . . No sins are small when committed against a great and generous God."[6]

We need forgiveness for all sin. For past, present, and future sin.

Now, if the penalty for sin is death, and if we all have a measure of sin in us, and if we are all violators, and God does not grade on a curve but instead holds us accountable to his perfect standard . . . what hope do we really have? The answer? Only through the cross do we find salvation. When the people to whom Peter was speaking on the Day of Pentecost heard this,

They were cut to the heart and said to Peter and the other apostles, "Brothers, what shall we do?"

Peter replied, "Repent and be baptized, every one of you, in the name of Jesus Christ for the forgiveness of your sins. And you will receive the gift of the Holy Spirit. The promise is for you and your children and for all who are far off—for all whom the Lord our God will call."

With many other words he warned them; and he pleaded with them, "Save yourselves from this corrupt generation." Those who accepted his message were baptized, and about three thousand were added to their number that day (Acts 2:37-41).

It's that simple. Peter said, "Repent and be baptized." That is the answer to "What shall we do?" And yet so many people throughout the history of the church just can't bring themselves to do it. Do you know why? Because most people look at their lives and say, "I'm not really that bad. I don't really need to . . . *repent.*"

REPENTANCE **IS HARD**

Early on a Saturday morning when Robin and I were living in Zimbabwe, a stranger drove up to the front of my house in a very expensive Mercedes. He got out of the car and exclaimed, "Father Jeff! [*He was Catholic and assumed I was as well.*] Can you please come to my house immediately? My mother is dying, and I want you to speak something over her, like last rites or something."

I thought, *Well, first of all, that's a Catholic thing,* but I didn't say that. I just agreed to go.

When we arrived, this man's entire family stood in the living room, weeping and desperately looking for someone who could rescue them from this predicament. They immediately marched me to the back corner of the house and closed the door behind me, leaving me alone with the tiny, frail, old woman who lay in her bed. I sat down beside her, grabbed her hand, and introduced myself. She was quiet, motionless, and seemingly unable to respond, so I doubted that any real dialogue could occur between us. But gently leaning toward her, I asked a simple question:

"Do you know Jesus?"

She said yes.

Then I said, "Has there ever been a time that you knelt at his cross and repented of your sins?"

Well, like a stick of ammonia into the nostrils of a prizefighter, that woke her up! She gave me a verbal lashing that I did not soon forget, and the only redeeming factor was that I didn't understand half of it. She did clearly convey, though, the idea of: "I'm no sinner! I have never hurt a soul! I've been a good person all my life! Now, young man, you can leave my room!"

Acknowledging sin and engaging in repentance are extremely difficult for a lot of people. Even those who are at death's door.

ILLUMINATION

Growing up in the eastern part of Tennessee, we enjoyed the occasional snowfall. Unfortunately, snow to Tennesseans is like rain to Californians—we have no idea how to drive in it. So when snow is forecast in Tennessee, the salt trucks load up and stand ready to douse the roads before the sun comes up. Salt gets everywhere! Problem is, when you pull out of your driveway early in the morning to go to work, you do not realize that a film of this rock salt has developed on your windshield.

> Most people look at their lives and say, "I'm not really that bad. I don't really need to . . . *repent.*

As long as it's dark outside, you can still see OK, because you're driving by your headlights. But when the sun starts to come out, the sunlight illuminates the rock salt, and all you can see is the film on your windshield. With visibility obstructed, car accidents start popping up everywhere. One after another after another after another . . . but there's no way you're going to get out and clean the windshield, because then you'd be cold! So the wrecks just keep happening!

John said that Jesus is the light that has come into the world (John 1:9). Through him we can see righteousness and unrighteousness. He illuminates the sin in our lives and opens our eyes to the truth of who we really are. When that happens we can respond in one of two ways:

First, we can harden our hearts. We can say, "Well, I know I feel convicted right now, but in reality, I don't need to repent. There are a lot of other people worse than me." When we begin rationalizing our own goodness, ignoring the light, a very bad thing happens. We can actually get to the point where our consciences become numb to the conviction of the Holy Spirit. Romans 1:21 says, "Although they knew God, they neither glorified him as God nor gave thanks to him, but their thinking became futile and their foolish hearts were darkened." A time will come when the light is no longer visible.

"Whoever conceals their sins does not prosper, but the one who confesses and renounces them finds mercy (Proverbs 28:13).

So the alternative to hardening our hearts is that we can RSVP to God's invitation. When Peter preached the first gospel sermon on the Day of Pentecost, the light came to more than three thousand people. They knew that something more was needed. They understood down deep inside that being good would never be good *enough*. Something was missing. So they asked, "What must we do?"

RSVP

Peter, under the direction of the Holy Spirit, challenged his audience to respond to God's invitation. In essence, he was reminding them that God, in Christ, had sent out an invite to all who would come. All they needed to do was "RSVP." And it's the same today.

R—REALIZE YOUR NEED

Accepting the truth that you cannot save yourself is the all-important first step into a right relationship with God. This is the identifying mark of a Christ follower. It is also that which distinguishes Christianity from the other major world religions. Those religions are not grace based, but works based. They include elements of measuring up, elements of earning merit, elements of *doing*. So while false religious systems emphasize the *do,* Jesus emphatically proclaims, "Done!" Everything that needed to be accomplished in order to make it possible for people to be right with God has already been done, two thousand years ago on the cross of Jesus Christ.

Only God can save us. Our sin separates us from the Creator, and no amount of moral effort will repair the damage and place us in a right relationship with God. This is precisely why Paul adores the gospel and is in no way ashamed of it—"because it is the power of God that brings salvation" (Romans 1:16).

Whose power saves you? God's power.

Not a little bit of God and a little bit of you.

God.

Full stop.

Paul insists that he is "not ashamed of the gospel . . . for in the gospel the righteousness of God is revealed" (vv. 16, 17). But how does God's righteousness save us? Knowing that we are incapable of living a perfect life, God paid our penalty for us by sending his Son to die on a cross, bearing all our sin and shame on his shoulders, justifying us before God and meeting the requirements of the law on our behalf. In essence, Jesus made us right with the law of God by paying the penalty and crediting that payment to our account.

S—SAY YOU'RE SORRY . . . AND MEAN IT

Part of repentance includes the realization that you have been going in the wrong direction. When Jesus opens your eyes to who you really are, a genuine sadness penetrates the soul. You begin to realize that your sins have wounded not only those around you but also the heart of God. A person who has encountered Jesus does an about-face and decides that he will live a new life. Jesus said, "Blessed are those who mourn, for they will be comforted" (Matthew 5:4). Those who weep over their sins will indeed be comforted by his forgiveness.

> You begin to realize that your sins have wounded not only those around you but also the heart of God.

Someone objects, "I thought you just said that everything that needed to be done for me to be right with God was accomplished on the cross of Jesus Christ two thousand years ago! Now you are saying I have to change my life as well?" Two responses must be given at this point.

First—"Grace," as Dallas Willard says, "is not opposed to effort. It is opposed to earning."[7] In other words, our desire to begin living in the opposite direction has nothing to do with an attempt to earn enough "goodness points" for entrance into Christ's kingdom. Rather, our effort to do the good originates from our appreciation for the salvation already provided and our understanding that the parameters Jesus sets for our lives are designed to bring the abundant life.

Second—and perhaps more crucial to this issue—when we repent of our sins and are baptized, the Bible says the Holy Spirit of God comes to live inside us, changing not only what we do but what we *want* to do. In other words, along with the forgiveness of sins, Jesus gives us the desire and power to live a righteous life by placing his Spirit within all those who have called on the name of the Lord. A passionate pursuit of godliness is the natural result of true conversion. In Acts 19:18, 19, for example, the people who decided to follow Jesus were moved to confess their sorcery *and* to destroy their occult objects. (Also see Galatians 2:20.)

> Christ followers in the first-century church proudly verbalized their commitment to Jesus. In fact, proclaiming or confessing the name of Jesus was not a painstaking exercise but, instead, the natural result of an authentic encounter with Jesus.

V—VERBALIZE YOUR COMMITMENT

Jesus was clear that if we confess his name before others, he will confess our names before the Father (Matthew 10:32). A commitment to Christ means exactly that—commitment. When we truly believe that without Jesus we are lost and resigned to an eternity without God, our appreciation for his work on the cross dramatically expresses itself in the way we live. We are in no way ashamed of Jesus. We proclaim his name at home, at school, at work, on the soccer field, and in the marketplace. Our friends do not have to guess why we live the way we live. If they have spent any amount of time with us, they know who we believe in, and they see our shamelessness concerning the name of Jesus.

Christ followers in the first-century church proudly verbalized their commitment to Jesus. In fact, proclaiming or confessing the name of Jesus was not a painstaking exercise but, instead, the natural result of an authentic encounter with Jesus. This explains Peter's response to those who held the power to execute him. When they demanded that he stop proclaiming the name of Jesus, Peter countered with, "We cannot help speaking about what we have seen and heard" (Acts 4:18-20). Authentic salvation always leads to a verbal proclamation and appreciation of what Christ has done. Thomas, the most famous doubter of all time, modeled this for us when he declared, "My Lord and my God!" (John 20:28).

P—PLUNGE YOUR PAST

When God entered into the old covenant relationship with his people, three things emerged:

1. circumcision
2. sacrifice
3. water cleansing

Jesus, the Son of God, was born a Jew and died for all, becoming a physical representation of the new covenant replacing the old—not to abolish the law of God, but to fulfill it.

For instance, where circumcision is concerned, the book of Romans says that a new kind of circumcision has come. "A person is not a Jew who is one only outwardly, nor is circumcision merely outward and physical. No, a person is a Jew who is one inwardly; and circumcision is circumcision of the heart, by the Spirit, not by the written code. Such a person's praise is not from other people, but from God" (Romans 2:28, 29).

So we are no longer required to circumcise the flesh; but God, through his Holy Spirit, circumcises our hearts. The change in us is much more dramatic than merely physical. Transformation has taken place in our spirit. It is no longer we who live but Christ who lives in us. Old desires fade. New desires surface with an extraordinary power to be what God has called us to be.

Now where sacrifice is concerned, some of my friends will say, "The God of the Old Testament is a bit frightening. What's all this about slaughtering animals and watching the blood trickle down the altar?"

My initial response is, "Good! I'm glad you're offended, because that's the whole point!" Sacrifices were instituted as a graphic reminder of the seriousness of sin. All sin brings death of some kind—spiritual, physical, and even emotional. Every time God's people brought an animal to the altar for sacrifice, they were reminded of this reality.

So God wants to enter into a new covenant with you and me. First, he requires circumcision of the heart. Second, he requires the sacrifice of his one and only Son. But notice that in both cases, what God requires, he provides.

Finally, he requires baptism. Again, even though baptism is first instituted in the New Testament, water cleansing began back in the Old Testament as a prerequisite to entering into a covenant relationship with God. Before Israel could meet God on the mountain and receive the Ten Commandments . . . "The LORD said to Moses, 'Go to the people and consecrate them today and tomorrow. Have them wash their clothes and be ready by the third day, because on that day the LORD will come down on Mount Sinai in the sight of all the people'" (Exodus 19:10, 11).

There had to be a cleansing.

And when we step into the waters of baptism, we are making preparation for God's Spirit to come live in us. Is this exciting or what? Paul said, "Don't you know that all of us who were baptized into Christ Jesus were baptized into his death? We were therefore buried with him through baptism into death in order that, just as Christ was raised from the dead through the glory of the Father, we too may live a new life" (Romans 6:3, 4).

Although there is nothing magical about the water, God sees our willingness to obey his command as a commitment to enter into a covenant relationship with him. In the waters of baptism God purifies us and makes us ready to receive his Spirit (Acts 2:38; see also 5:32; 1 John 5:3).

There are three things you see with every baptism in the early church as recorded in the book of Acts:

1. Baptism was done immediately, with no waiting period.
2. Baptism was done in response to God's command. People didn't sit around and have great theological debates about whether or not baptism saves you. God said to do it, so they just did it!
3. It was done by those who believed the gospel. The prerequisite to baptism was the belief and affirmation that God had designated the cross of Jesus Christ as the avenue through which forgiveness of sin comes. Notice the response of Philip's audience: "When they believed Philip as he proclaimed the good news of the kingdom of God and the name of Jesus Christ, they were baptized, both men and women. Simon himself believed and was baptized. And he followed Philip everywhere, astonished by the great signs and miracles he saw" (Acts 8:12, 13).

Baptism is done immediately. Baptism is a response to a direct command from God for those who believe. Baptism is where we die to our old way of living and rise to a new way of life. One who truly wants to follow Jesus will plunge the past.

BRINGING IT **ALL TOGETHER**

It's important to understand the meaning of the promise "I will save you" for several reasons:

1. In order to know how (and by whom) that promise can be claimed.

2. In order to appreciate and be grateful about what we are being saved *from* (eternal damnation, a life enslaved to sin . . .).
3. In order to have a solid understanding of what that promise *isn't* about. It's not about being saved from trouble or hardship—the Christian life is not one of laziness, but one of action.

Many people feel that if God really does exist and is as loving as Christians claim he is, then he should just forgive everyone and call us all into Heaven at the end of time. These people understand only one side of God's nature—love. However, the Bible portrays God's essence as including both holiness (1 Peter 1:16) and love (1 John 4:8, 16). In other words, everything that is holy, pure, and righteous, God is. Moreover, all that is included in love—mercy, grace, acceptance, compassion . . . all of it—exudes from the nature and character of God as well. So when sin enters into the picture, a tension exists between the love of God and the holiness of God.

God's holiness requires him to punish our sin, but God's love greatly motivates him to forgive it. This is a precarious position. How can God remain true to both his holiness and his love? If he simply forgives us, then his holiness will be violated. If he gives us the wages of our sin—death—his love will be stifled and his mercy left unexpressed.

Thank God! He provided a way to meet both sides of his nature. How? By sending his own Son to die on a cross. When Jesus died on the cross, he met the requirements of God's holiness by paying the penalty for our sins. Second Corinthians 5:21 states, "God made him who had no sin to be sin for us, so that in him we might become the righteousness of God." This, more than anything else, should remove any and all doubt that God's love is deeper and wider than we could ever imagine, and he was willing to do whatever it takes to save us.

Moreover, Jesus' death on the cross—etched into history for all the world to see—successfully communicated to the entire human race the measure and intensity of God's love for all mankind. The invitation is for everyone: "To all who did receive him, to those who believed in his name, he gave the right to become children of God" (John 1:12).

The promise "I will save you" is about having "life in his name" (John 20:31). No other promise holds greater significance.

GREAT AND PRECIOUS PROMISES

FOR INDIVIDUAL OR GROUP STUDY

God in his grace promises a way for anyone to be saved from the consequence of sin (eternal death). When we come to faith in Jesus Christ and his death on the cross, we are in a position to repent of sin and be baptized. Baptism is a picture and profession of Jesus' death, burial, and resurrection. When we follow through in obedience, the Holy Spirit takes up residence in our lives.

1 Recall a time when you or someone you know was rescued from a life-threatening situation. What happened? How long ago was this? What, if anything, was done to thank/repay the person for the rescue? Has the feeling of gratitude faded with time? Why or why not?

2 Do you see yourself as a good person? Why? Are you ever tempted to think that you can earn God's favor by being more good than bad? Explain.

3 Have you sent in your RSVP to God's invitation? If so, how has your life changed? Have you verbalized your commitment? Do your family, friends, and coworkers know you're a Christian? Why or why not?

4 Have you ever suspected that someone's claim of being "saved" wasn't entirely true? Why? In your opinion, what are signs of a person's acceptance of Jesus as Savior? How do you think *your* story would hold up if others evaluated your life by the same criteria?

5 Why is it important to understand what God's promise to save us means? How would you describe the act of God's saving us—is it a one-time event in our lives or an ongoing exercise? Explain your answers.

CHAPTER FIVE

I WILL
ANSWER YOU
ACTS 16:22-34

O N JULY 19, 1989, the captain of United Airlines flight 232 announced over the loudspeaker that an emergency landing was inevitable.[1] The DC-10 aircraft's tail engine had failed, causing total hydraulic failure. Jeff Miller, a young businessman, was on that plane. What do you think went through his mind in those moments before the plane he was on crashed into an Iowa cornfield? Undoubtedly he asked God to save him. Some would say God answered.

Jeff was one of the 183 passengers who survived the crash. The right wing of the plane hit the ground first, causing the plane to cartwheel and rip apart into a giant fireball. Jeff's piece of the plane broke off, tumbling over and coming to an abrupt stop in the field. There he found himself, still strapped in his seat, hanging upside down—but alive and unharmed!

When you are in deep trouble and you know the only one who can save you is God, what do you do? You pray! Christian or not, people who are in dire situations call on God to save them. It's an amazing thing, really. I can preach hundreds of sermons on prayer, but the times I see my congregation really start praying are when the rug gets pulled out from under them in some area (finances, marriage, children, job, health). Trouble comes, and suddenly we start praying harder! The more intense the trouble, the more intense the prayers.

Jesus, who often went to his Father in prayer, understood about trouble. He was troubled in his own heart while he lived on this earth (Matthew 26:37;

Mark 14:33; John 11:33; 12:27; 13:21), and during those times, he prayed. He also warned his disciples of the trouble they would experience, at the same time giving them the reason they could go to him for help: "I have told you these things, so that in me you may have peace. In this world you will have trouble. But take heart! I have overcome the world" (John 16:33).

Every trip around the sun brings challenges, dangers, and potential hazards —some we know about and some we don't. So rather than praying only when we sense danger or trouble, prayer should be the posture of our lives. Jesus has overcome the world—surely we can trust him with more times than just the dark ones? When we call on the Lord Jesus, at any time, he promises he will answer: "Very truly I tell you, my Father will give you whatever you ask in my name. Until now you have not asked for anything in my name. Ask and you will receive, and your joy will be complete" (vv. 23, 24).

Like all of us who live on this earth, the apostle Paul was no stranger to trouble. But you might come to think that his *view* of trouble was pretty strange. In his letter to the Christians in Corinth, he wrote: "We do not want you to be uninformed, brothers and sisters, about the troubles we experienced in the province of Asia. We were under great pressure, far beyond our ability to endure, so that we despaired of life itself. Indeed, we felt we had received the sentence of death. But this happened that we might not rely on ourselves but on God, who raises the dead" (2 Corinthians 1:8, 9). Later he also said: "Though outwardly we are wasting away, yet inwardly we are being renewed day by day. For our light and momentary troubles are achieving for us an eternal glory that far outweighs them all" (4:16, 17). And Paul often spoke of sharing in the sufferings of Christ, as in his letter to the Romans: "Now if we are children, then we are heirs—heirs of God and co-heirs with Christ, if indeed we share in his sufferings in order that we may also share in his glory" (8:17).

Paul didn't just *suffer* for Christ; he seemed to welcome, or even invite, this suffering. That's exactly the situation we see when Paul and Silas went to Philippi. According to Acts 16, Paul and Silas (on their way to a prayer meeting, incidentally) encountered a young slave girl engaged in a sort of fortune-telling, by which she was bringing in good money for her masters (v. 16). For some unknown reason, the slave girl began following Paul and Silas and proclaiming that they were servants of "the Most High God." Furthermore, she affirmed that the apostles were telling the people "the way to be saved" (v. 17).

We are not told why Paul put up with this for several days. (Perhaps he was hoping to avoid the charge of disturbing the peace, or perhaps he was simply busy with more urgent issues.) But eventually he cast out the evil spirit (v. 18). This was offensive to the slave girl's owners. No more evil spirit meant no more money. Therefore, they complained to the authorities that Paul and Silas were encouraging civil unrest (vv. 20, 21). A crowd joined in support of these false charges, so Paul and Silas were stripped, beaten, and thrown into prison (vv. 22, 23).

That wasn't the first time Paul had ended up in trouble while spreading the gospel message, nor would it be the last.

Pause for a moment.

Imagine that you are Paul or Silas. You've been beaten and arrested on trumped-up charges. You know you could declare your citizenship and be let out at any time. It's been an unusually awful day. So what do you do?

> Like all of us who live on this earth, the apostle Paul was no stranger to trouble.

You hold a worship service for the prisoners, of course! "About midnight Paul and Silas were praying and singing hymns to God, and the other prisoners were listening to them" (v. 25). Have you ever considered what they might have been asking God for? What would *you* pray for? Rescue? Revenge on those slave owners? An earthquake?

WHAT ARE YOU ASKING FOR?

Sometimes the reason we don't see God's answers in our lives is that we haven't even begun with the right question. Or perhaps we asked for something without really thinking about what the answer could involve.

Jeff Miller sat on that plane and cried out for God's help. We can look at the results of his landing unharmed and think he got his answer. But more than a hundred other passengers on the plane died that day. Did Jeff ask God to save him and kill a hundred other people? No, certainly not. What about those other passengers? Did they just not ask God for help?

James 5:16 assures us that "the prayer of a righteous person is powerful and effective." So are we to say then that Jeff Miller was righteous and the rest of the people on that plane were not? And does God answer only the prayers of the righteous?

Let's look again at that verse in the fuller context, James 5:13-18, and see what James is saying:

Is anyone among you in trouble? Let them pray. Is anyone happy? Let them sing songs of praise. Is anyone among you sick? Let them call the elders of the church to pray over them and anoint them with oil in the name of the Lord. And the prayer offered in faith will make the sick person well; the Lord will raise them up. If they have sinned, they will be forgiven. Therefore confess your sins to each other and pray for each other so that you may be healed. The prayer of a righteous person is powerful and effective.

Elijah was a human being, even as we are. He prayed earnestly that it would not rain, and it did not rain on the land for three and a half years. Again he prayed, and the heavens gave rain, and the earth produced its crops.

James tells us we should pray in trouble, in sickness, and when we are in the wrong. But in none of these cases does the healing come because of the status of the people praying—you don't have to be a supersaint to come to God with your requests. It is the *Lord* who raises people up, who forgives, and who heals—not the righteous man or woman. The prayer of a righteous person is powerful because that person knows to call on the power of God. The prayer of a righteous person is effective because God is the one who effects the result.

> Every time I read this story, I wonder why God didn't just destroy Jezebel and the false prophets and be done with it.

No doubt we all know of people of great faith who pray and seem to receive powerful answers. But I think this has more to do with the fact that when you are striving to live a righteous life, a life built on a strong faith, you become more intimately aware of where and how God is working in your life and in the lives of others. You learn to listen better for what God wants, and to allow him to shape your desires to be more like his. So when you ask, you ask for the very things God is wanting to happen. Thus, your prayers are powerful and effective.

Elijah, the example James provided, was indeed just a man. But he was a man who served God. He did not ask for that rain to stop and to come again on his own whims. He asked for what God wanted to happen.

ELIJAH ASKED, **GOD ANSWERED**

Elijah's story is a bit more intriguing than just those few lines recorded in the fifth chapter of James. When we first meet Elijah, Ahab is king over Israel. We are told that, as a king, "Ahab son of Omri did more evil in the eyes of the LORD than any of those before him" (1 Kings 16:30). That's quite a line, because the preceding chapters of the Bible convey no shortage of evil among Ahab's predecessors. Yet the new king seemed intent on taking evil to a new level.

Ahab married Jezebel, the daughter of an enemy king and a worshipper of Baal (v. 31). Then he had the audacity to establish an altar to Baal within the temple of God (probably to appease Jezebel, because all of us men know the motto we live by: "If Mama ain't happy, ain't nobody happy"). Finally, to add insult to injury, Ahab put his wife in charge of religion in the entire kingdom, and Jezebel wanted to do one thing and one thing only: she wanted to replace the worship of God with the worship of Baal. So she killed all God's prophets that she could find. That's right. She rounded up God's messengers and slaughtered them—but Elijah was safely tucked away out in the desert.

But before this killing spree started, Elijah was obedient to God and stood before Ahab, telling him that "there will be neither dew nor rain in the next few years except at my word" (17:1). Then God sent his servant Elijah out into the desert to be fed by ravens.

Every time I read this story, I wonder why God didn't just destroy Jezebel and the false prophets and be done with it. Ever think about that? Sometimes God seems to do things in a roundabout way. Why would a prophet of God ever have to run and hide? I mean, he served the Most High God, right? He had the Holy Spirit bubble of protection around him, right? Why didn't God just wipe the floor with King Ahab, Queen Jezebel, and the false prophets?

God promises to answer when we call, but we don't always get the full answer in one dose. Healing, rather than happening instantaneously, often comes over a period of time. God's intervention often comes not quickly and overpoweringly but, rather, slowly and effectively over the long haul. Why?

I make no claim to an exhaustive or complete answer to this dilemma. We are finite creatures living in a world created by the Infinite. There will always be a limit to our understanding. However, a limited understanding is different from having no understanding at all. For instance, perhaps the reason God did not destroy King Ahab, Queen Jezebel, and company is the same reason he does not destroy you and me when we willfully sin against him. God is the God of grace, mercy, kindness, and longsuffering. The heart of God longs for repentance from his people. Had Ahab or Jezebel repented at any time during this confrontation, God would have been quick to forgive.

> The prophets of Baal shouted and danced and even cut themselves, from morning to afternoon. But they got nothing.

King Ahab and I have something in common then. Both of us have had moments when we deliberately disobeyed God. Therefore, both of us desperately need God's grace and mercy. Funny how I think I deserve such grace but am quick to want God's judgment to come down hard and fierce on Jezebel and her idol-making husband. Of course Jezebel's actions were outrageous, horrible, and atrocious—but not unforgivable.

As to the question concerning God's roundabout way, a careful reading of the Scriptures indicates that often God seems as much interested in the process as he is in the final product. Elijah found himself depending on the ravens for his food and a stream for his water, both supplied by God. Then God sent him to the home of an impoverished widow on the Mediterranean coast—a widow who, through a miracle, was able to prepare enough food for both Elijah and her small family. Every day the widow had just enough food in the cupboard for that day's provision, requiring day-by-day dependence on God.

But the dramatic test of faith came on the day Elijah faced the 450 prophets of Baal and the 400 prophets of Asherah (1 Kings 18:16-46). "If the LORD is God, follow him; but if Baal is God, follow him," Elijah challenged the people (v. 21). Then he set up the test. Two bulls would be selected for the offering. Each would be cut up and placed on wood for a fire, but not set alight. "Then you call on the name of your god, and I will call on the name of the LORD. The god who answers by fire—he is God" (v. 24).

Perhaps you've heard this story. Even if you haven't, you might guess the end result. The prophets of Baal shouted and danced and even cut themselves, from morning to afternoon. But they got nothing. Then Elijah had water poured on his altar. One, two, three times, large jars of water were poured out on the offering and the wood, until the water pooled around the altar in a trench Elijah had dug himself. Then he prayed: "Answer me, LORD, answer me, so these people will know that you, LORD, are God, and that you are turning their hearts back again" (v. 37).

And this time the one true God answered, just as Elijah had said, by fire. That fire came down, burned the sacrifice, burned the stones, burned the wood, burned the dust, and licked up all the water in the trench. When you call on the name of God—the real God—the God of Abraham, Isaac, and Jacob, he answers every time, and his answer is both powerful and effective.

But even this fiery show was not enough to change the heart of Jezebel. She vowed to hunt Elijah down and take his life. Elijah ran for his life, and once again the Lord provided for him (1 Kings 19:1-9). Then God gave Elijah a very special gift—the gift of his presence: "Then a great and powerful wind tore the mountains apart and shattered the rocks before the LORD, but the LORD was not in the wind. After the wind there was an earthquake, but the LORD was not in the earthquake. After the earthquake came a fire, but the LORD was not in the fire. And after the fire came a gentle whisper. When Elijah heard it, he pulled his cloak over his face and went out and stood at the mouth of the cave.

"Then a voice said to him, 'What are you doing here, Elijah?'" (vv. 11-13).

NOT IN **THE EARTHQUAKE**

God often answers us in ways we don't understand—ways we would never choose if we were God:

- a talking donkey
- a strange dream
- a prostitute's shelter
- a gentle whisper
- a baby in a manger
- a crucified King . . .

Let's go back to another unlikely scene of God's presence, and other unlikely servants of God—Paul, the former persecutor, and his partner in crime, Silas. When we last left them, they were still in prison, singing praises and praying.

This, of course, is not the first prison scene in the book of Acts. Those apostles were known troublemakers. In Acts 4 we find Peter and John thrown into prison. Through some compelling speeches and the even more compelling voice of the crowds, they were released (vv. 1-22). They rejoined their people and reported on all that had happened. Then they all prayed together: "Now, Lord, consider their threats and enable your servants to speak your word with great boldness. Stretch out your hand to heal and perform signs and wonders through the name of your holy servant Jesus" (vv. 29, 30).

After they prayed, what happened? An earthquake. "The place where they were meeting was shaken. And they were all filled with the Holy Spirit and spoke the word of God boldly" (v. 31).

Though the shaking is what grabs our attention, the Lord's answer wasn't the earthquake. His answer to their prayer came in their ability to speak the word of God boldly through the Holy Spirit.

In another account the apostles were arrested and put in jail—due once again to the jealousy of the Jewish leaders. This time an angel came to their rescue. The angel appearance is amazing—and distracting. We might miss that God's answer to their prayers wasn't the angel. His answer was an opportunity for them to go and "tell the people all about this new life" (Acts 5:20).

And that is what they did. And once again they were seized and brought before the Jewish authorities. But this time a Pharisee named Gamaliel provided the answer, in words that echo Elijah's challenge to the prophets of Baal: "Leave these men alone! Let them go! For if their purpose or activity is of human origin, it will fail. But if it is from God, you will not be able to stop these men; you will only find yourselves fighting against God" (vv. 38, 39). Luke tells us that the apostles actually left the Sanhedrin that day, rejoicing "because they had been counted worthy of suffering disgrace for the Name" (v. 41).

Paul and Silas were of one mind with these followers of Jesus. They were not concerned about leaving the prison that night—as might be our first instinct. They rejoiced in the opportunity they had for the name of Christ. So if they were not asking for an earthquake to break them free, what did they ask for?

FOUNDATIONS SHAKEN

A clue might be found in Paul's letter to the Philippians. Paul wrote from prison (a different prison than the one in Acts 16): "Now I want you to know, brothers and sisters, that what has happened to me has actually served to advance the gospel. As a result, it has become clear throughout the whole palace guard and to everyone else that I am in chains for Christ. And because of my chains, most of the brothers and sisters have become confident in the Lord and dare all the more to proclaim the gospel without fear" (Philippians 1:12-14). Later he encouraged his audience: "Therefore, my dear friends, as you have always obeyed—not only in my presence, but now much more in my absence—continue to work out your salvation with fear and trembling, for it is God who works in you to will and to act in order to fulfill his good purpose" (2:12, 13).

Paul wanted people to tremble, but not from the ground shaking. He wanted their souls to be shaken up so they could find the way to salvation. He wanted an opportunity to spread the message of the gospel to anyone who would listen. It was as the demon-possessed slave girl had said—these men were telling the people the way to be saved. They were doing that within the prison walls just as much as they did on the outside.

> They were not concerned about leaving the prison
> that night—as might be our first instinct.

So when the earthquake shook the foundation of the prison and the chains and doors were broken, allowing all the prisoners the chance to be set free, no one escaped. Why? The freedom they wanted was not outside, but in the words of Paul and Silas. Seeing that these men had something amazing about them, the bewildered jailer rushed in and fell before Paul and Silas, trembling on the ground. But he did not ask them what happened or why they were still there. He asked them, "What must I do to be saved?" (Acts 16:30). Within hours, the jailer's entire household was baptized and began a new life in Christ (vv. 31-33).

We call. God answers. Things happen.

This is the story of my own life and the lives of hundreds of people with whom I have shared stories. When the odds are so heavily stacked against me and I know the only way out of my predicament is God, something interesting happens. My prayer life intensifies. My willingness to go to God seems greater. My desire to be in the presence of God goes to another level. Alternatively, if I call on God and he powers up and immediately delivers me from my circumstances, my gratitude may be intense for the moment, but my passion for him soon fades.

Day-by-day dependence on God results in priceless treasures. This is why I believe God is just as much interested in the process as he is in the final product. Intimacy with God comes as a result of time spent with him. Trust soon develops as we begin to see how God has helped us clear each hurdle in the past. This leads to faith in the promise of God that when we call on him in the future, he will be faithful to answer every single time.

FRIEDA **CALLED**

Recently, I met an angel. Her name is Frieda. Having been diagnosed with breast cancer, she is fighting the battle of her life. Frieda sat across the table from my wife and me, wearing a beautiful white hat to cover up the effects of the chemo. Her smile was radiant and her personality pleasant and contagious. My wife had told me that I should take the time to meet Frieda because "she's the most amazing woman I have ever seen." As soon as I sat down, I saw a face filled with joy and delight.

She spoke and I listened (a rarity for preachers) for over half an hour. She kept saying how Jesus had revealed himself to her in a very special way over the last few months. No one is glad to be diagnosed with this horrible disease, but there was a part of Frieda that seemed glad to be in the middle of this battle. No, she was not in denial. She was well aware of the uncertainty and possible terminality of her disease. Speaking openly concerning the painful chemotherapy treatments, Frieda described how her husband had held her in his arms through an unbearable night of suffering.

Changing the subject back to Jesus, however, she spoke of how God had given her a vision and a dream whereby she (not unlike the lady in Luke 8 who had been subject to bleeding) kept reaching out for Jesus in order to touch the hem of his garment that she might be healed.

"And in my dream," she said, "I can see Jesus reaching out to me. Jesus has shown me that he is here and has never left me and he will give me the strength I need to make it through the pain. And when I need him, all I have to do is call, and he will answer."

Listening to Frieda reminded me of Peter Kreeft's comments concerning pain and the skeptic: "It is significant to note that most of the objections to the existence of God from the problem of suffering come from outside observers who are quite comfortable, whereas those who actually do the suffering are made into stronger believers by their suffering."[2]

True, isn't it? Those who suffer the most do seem to know God best.

When we call, God answers, but he answers in a way that brings relationship, intimacy, trust, and faith—faith in him *and* in his ability to give us what we need to fight the battles of our lives. We can rejoice in suffering because through it we come to know the God of the universe in a way we may never have. It's not the kind of knowledge that comes in an earthquake or in fire from the sky. It's the kind of knowledge that begins by knowing him through his Word and that grows through the process of digging out of the rubble or running through the desert.

LIVING WITH THE ANSWER

When Jeff Miller found himself staring at the ceiling of the plane, thanking God for his life, he saw one thing—his Bible. Jeff left that plane crash a new person, changed by the realization that life can be taken from you at a moment's notice. But the new life he took hold of came through day-by-day dependence on the God he knew. He went on to speak at churches and community meetings and other events, telling about his survival and about his new perspective.

> "Do not be anxious about anything, but in every situation, by prayer and petition, with thanksgiving, present your requests to God."

Though we know about how Paul and Silas went on to keep telling the message of Christ and salvation after this prison episode, we don't know what later happened to the jailer or to the prisoners who were there that night, listening to these men telling the way to salvation. But it's safe to say that the jailer probably took every opportunity to tell anyone who would listen about his new life in Christ. Think of all the people who may have passed through those prison gates and been affected by this man's testimony!

Perhaps he was still there in Philippi on the day Paul's letter was read. If so, he would have surely latched on to these words: "Do not be anxious about anything, but in every situation, by prayer and petition, with thanksgiving, present your requests to God. And the peace of God, which transcends all understanding, will guard your hearts and your minds in Christ Jesus" (Philippians 4:6, 7).

ASK THE GOD WHO ANSWERS

The message in the Bible is simple and clear: When we, the people of God, call out to him, he answers. When we are in trouble, he answers. But the answer he gives may not always be rescue. We need to stay close to God, to keep talking to him, to keep asking him questions, even when our flight is smooth. When we actually believe that the same God who said, "Let there be light" . . . who said, "Be still" to the winds and the waves . . . who held the sun in the sky . . . who enabled young David to slay the giant Goliath . . . is the same God who is in our corner, we will pray. When we actually believe that he is able to do much more than we ever ask for, hope for, or imagine, we will pray and pray some more.

His answer may transcend all our understanding, but there is one thing we can know for certain: when we call on his name, he will always answer.

GREAT AND PRECIOUS PROMISES

FOR INDIVIDUAL OR GROUP STUDY

Throughout this chapter and, in fact, throughout this book, we have highlighted the reality that there are some questions for which we may never have complete and exhaustive answers. However, some certainties do indeed exist. One, when we call on God he always answers. Two, he may not give us the answer for which we were hoping, but his answer is always the right answer where kingdom advancement is concerned. Finally, we must trust that he will sustain us and give us what we need during those times that the answers he gives require us to live day by day under his provision.

1 Describe a time when you called on God and he answered in a dramatic fashion. How did that make you feel? How did it impact the way you see God?

2 Describe, if you can, a time when you called on God and his answer was *not* the one you had hoped for or expected. How did that make you feel? How did it impact your understanding of God?

3 Describe a time when you called on God and he answered, but his answer was no. Did you find yourself losing faith and trust in God? Explain your answer.

4 Describe, if you can, a time when you called on God to take something away or grant you a special desire or move in a dramatic way, but instead, God moved very slowly and seemingly in a day-to-day fashion. What was your response? Did you grow closer to God during that time? Explain. How did your prayer life change? How did you notice God working in your life?

5 What is the difference between saying "God always answers when we call" and "God always gives us what we ask for"?

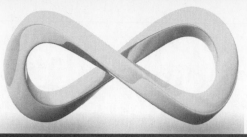

CHAPTER SIX

I WILL
FORGIVE YOU
ROMANS 6:1-7

FORGIVENESS IS A PRECIOUS thing. In fact, of all the promises God graciously gives in his Word, "I will forgive" (see Jeremiah 31:34, for example) is the most profound because it is the one that resonates most with our hearts. Yet it is the one promise we find most difficult to make to others.

Edith Taylor was living in Waltham, Massachusetts, during the World War II era.[1] She had found the love of her life and anticipated growing old with the man of her dreams. Edith settled in, started a family, and looked forward to writing many chapters of the book of marital bliss.

For a few years, things went along as planned. Then her husband's job took him overseas. Separated by a great distance, letters of love passed frequently between them. The children desperately missed their father, and Edith longed to be reunited with her husband.

Then the letters slowed down. And one day a letter came that broke Edith's heart. One can only imagine the devastation she felt when she discovered that her husband had met a Japanese girl and was beginning a new life with her. He spoke of new dreams and a new family in a new country that would now become his home.

Edith was shattered. But over the next few years, she tried to keep a connection to her former husband, at least partly for her children's sake. Some letters, photographs, and gifts went back and forth. Each time Edith opened a new letter or viewed photos of the new family, her heart was broken all over again.

Then Edith received a letter from her husband, informing her that he was terminally ill. Some versions of the story say that the husband asked Edith to care for his family; other versions say that Edith offered. Either way, what a cruel twist—that the discarded wife should provide for her husband's second family!

But that is exactly what Edith did.

Edith found a way to forgive her husband, his mistress, and the whole adulterous affair. And eventually, two little children and their mother moved in with Edith. Edith was by no means wealthy. The years of giving assistance to a woman who in no way deserved her mercy, coupled with caring for children who demanded great sacrifices, would exhaust every bit of her energy and finances. Yet willingly, graciously, and even joyfully, she did what needed to be done.

How could she muster up the courage, grace, mercy—and forgiveness—required to do what she did? I find her explanation compelling: "In that dark, dreary, hellish situation, I thank God for the ray of light and hope to share some of the love of God in this very dismal setting."

Forgiveness is a beautiful, if not awesome and mind-boggling, thing! When you are on the receiving end, it can save your life. Thank God, forgiveness is the promise God makes to all who call on his name (see 2 Chronicles 7:14, for example). When it comes to forgiveness, there are usually four types of people:

- those who think they don't need forgiveness
- those who abuse forgiveness
- those who believe that forgiveness is too good to be true
- those who humbly embrace forgiveness

THOSE WHO THINK THEY **DON'T NEED FORGIVENESS**

A college student asked to meet with me after I had preached a weekend message on sin and salvation. Standing in our church café, he accused me of creating a false need and then providing a solution to meet that need.

"Salvation," he complained, "is only relevant if one is in need of saving."

I said, "Well, the Bible says that we are all sinners and that the wages of sin is death." (See Romans 3:23; 6:23.)

His response? "Well, I would agree that I am not perfect, but I don't see myself as a sinner."

"What do you see yourself as?" I asked back.

"A good person who occasionally does bad things."

The conversation continued until I challenged his idea. If he is a good person who occasionally does bad things, I suggested, then why not just stop doing bad things? Simply wake up tomorrow and decide that you are never going to tell another lie, think a bad thought, or covet what does not belong to you. In fact, just decide that from now on, you will never again do anything wrong.

He said, "That's impossible."

I said, "That's right. And do you know why? Because you are a sinner. You are not a good person who occasionally does bad things. Instead, you are a bad person who occasionally does good things."[2]

Indeed, the heart of man is wicked and deceitful (Jeremiah 17:9). In fact, even when we do the right things, our motivation is often impure. The Bible makes no exceptions to the list of sinners (besides Jesus—2 Corinthians 5:21). All have sinned because all are sinners and in desperate need of forgiveness.

So . . . we are all sinners. What's the big deal?

> Even when we do the right things, our motivation is often impure.

Well, all sin is a violation against a holy God. This holy God is required to separate himself from all sin. That means separation from you and me because we are all sinners. A totally perfect, righteous, and pure God does not have fellowship with unrighteousness. We have committed cosmic treason. Thank God that, through Jesus, a path to forgiveness has been laid out before us. God's desire is not to condemn (John 3:16, 17); he provides a way for us to cross over "from death to life" (John 5:24). The problem is, there are still many who believe that forgiveness is not something they need.

THOSE WHO **ABUSE FORGIVENESS**

During the last fifteen years of my ministry, I have noticed a growing trend. Many people do indeed see themselves as needing forgiveness. However, once they receive it, they abuse it. This is by no means an entirely new attitude toward forgiveness. The apostle Paul dealt with a similar attitude among the

Christians in Rome. In fact, he had to remind them that salvation (forgiveness) always leads to sanctification (a changed life). Paul wrote:

What shall we say, then? Shall we go on sinning so that grace may increase? By no means! We are those who have died to sin; how can we live in it any longer? Or don't you know that all of us who were baptized into Christ Jesus were baptized into his death? We were therefore buried with him through baptism into death in order that, just as Christ was raised from the dead through the glory of the Father, we too may live a new life.

For if we have been united with him in a death like his, we will certainly also be united with him in a resurrection like his. For we know that our old self was crucified with him so that the body ruled by sin might be done away with, that we should no longer be slaves to sin— because anyone who has died has been set free from sin (Romans 6:1-7).

Paul's charge is clear; his analogy, effective.

- How can anyone who has been on the receiving end of the largest grace operation in history continue to willfully sin?
- How can anyone who truly understands the cost of forgiveness found through the cross continue flippantly in a life of sin?
- How can anyone who genuinely comprehends the damage that sin causes the human race make no effort to cease and desist?

NEW POWER

Paul's greatest argument concerns the power, or effect, that authentic forgiveness catalyzes in the life of a true convert. He says, "If we have been united with him in a death like his, we will certainly also be united with him in a resurrection like his" (Romans 6:5).

The body Jesus possessed after his resurrection was and is much more powerful than his previous human body. It is perhaps the greatest before-and-after ever demonstrated. And of course, we will receive new bodies, resurrection bodies, when the time comes.

But does this not also illustrate what happens to us in this life when we accept God's forgiveness? We die to our old way of living and are resurrected to a new way of life. There is a new power in us. Before, the spirit was willing but the flesh was weak. Now, through Christ, the spirit is willing and the flesh is able.

Later in Romans 6 Paul says, "Do not offer any part of yourself to sin as an instrument of wickedness, but rather offer yourselves to God as those who have been brought from death to life; and offer every part of yourself to him as an instrument of righteousness" (v. 13). We will never reach perfection this side of Heaven, but we can choose to say no to sin when it asks to use our eyes, ears, mouth, feet, and any other part of our bodies.

Imagine two Mr. Potato Heads side by side. One is fully equipped. The eyes, ears, nose, and mouth—as well as the moustache—are all set in place. The other one is just a naked potato. The way I read Paul's words, if we ever hope to defeat the sin in our lives, we must see sin as a separate entity—one that needs our permission to fulfill its evil plan. Once we have humbled ourselves at the cross, forgiveness is ours; and God injects us with the power to say no to the naked potato (sin) when he demands to use our eyes, ears, mouth, or any other body part for his deceitful purposes.

NEW MASTER

We are no longer slaves to sin. We do not have to obey sin. We have a new master! When we are aware that we belong to God and when we acknowledge him as Lord and master, we should be motivated to exercise discipline, effort, and commitment toward defeating the destructive habits in our lives.

When I was a student at Johnson Bible College (now Johnson University), it was rare to go more than three or four chapel services without a speaker using the story of Charles Blondin to illustrate commitment.[3] In the mid-1800s Blondin walked on a hemp tightrope across Niagara Falls from the Canadian to the American side a total of seventeen different times. Can you imagine his concentration, discipline, and commitment? Tony Campolo, in his book *Let Me Tell You a Story*, recounts the legend of the time Blondin once paused on the American side and shouted, "I am Blondin! Do you believe in me?"

The crowd responded by screaming, "We believe! We believe!"

Blondin then asked, "Do you believe that I can go back across the falls on that tightrope carrying someone on my shoulders?"

Again the crowd yelled, "We believe! We believe!"

Blondin then asked, "Who will be that human being?"

There was dead silence.

Saying you are committed is entirely different from living as if you actually *are* committed. Yet a life of total commitment is the life to which Jesus calls us. It is a "give it all or don't give at all" calling. The high cost of forgiveness should remind us that where a renunciation of sin is concerned, no halfhearted effort is acceptable.

Grace and forgiveness through the cross are wonderful things. But the calling on our lives is to continue to grasp what it means to know Jesus, to come to a greater knowledge of him (see Philippians 3:7-14). Anyone sincerely doing that wouldn't be looking for a way to dodge his path. Ours is a journey of tightrope walking: straying neither "to the right or to the left" of God's way (Joshua 1:7), centered on Christ and his will for every area of our lives.

Unfortunately, many see grace and forgiveness as a license to sin. While serving in New Zealand, I met a middle-aged man who loved to debate everything. At first I found him interesting and intellectually stimulating. Then one Sunday after church he announced to me that he was moving in with his girlfriend to start a family. When I challenged him with the Bible's view concerning sex outside of marriage, he flippantly responded by saying, "Jesus forgave all my sins at the cross, so I am sure he will forgive this too." He neither challenged my interpretation of Scripture nor made any attempt to rationalize his sinful behavior. He knew his actions were wrong but viewed the cross as a sort of "get out of jail free card" to be utilized at his convenience.

> We will never reach perfection this side of Heaven, but we can choose to say no to sin when it asks to use our eyes, ears, mouth, feet, and any other part of our bodies.

Similarly, a few months ago, while surfing my Facebook pages, I saw risqué photos of a young man who had recently been baptized. I could not believe that a Christ follower would post provocative photos of himself in an attempt to attract women. As with the other man, when I challenged him on the issue, he made no attempt to justify his actions or to argue that what he had done was acceptable for a Christian. Instead, he simply said that Jesus would forgive him and that "I have to do what I have to do."

So some people seem to be saying, "Well, if my past, present, and future sins have been forgiven, then why should I walk the rope? Walking the rope is hard, risky, and requires lots of practice. Isn't it more comfortable just to cheer from the ground—and a lot safer? They fail to recognize who Jesus is and what he has done . . . and how dangerous and destructive sin really is, to those around us and to ourselves.

When I meet someone who claims to be a Christ follower but possesses a casual attitude toward sin, I can't help wondering if a genuine conversion has taken place. When the Holy Spirit of God comes to live inside us, we see things we have never seen, feel things we have never felt, do things we have never done. Christ's promise to forgive our sin is followed by the power to overcome it. Colossians 3:9, 10 says that "you have taken off your old self with its practices and have put on the new self." Galatians 2:20 says, "I have been crucified with Christ and I no longer live, but Christ lives in me." If Christ truly lives in us, a passion to expel the sin within becomes a present reality. We have been "set free from sin" (Romans 6:7).

THOSE WHO BELIEVE THAT FORGIVENESS IS **TOO GOOD TO BE TRUE**

There are those who think they don't need to be forgiven. There are those who abuse forgiveness. Then there are those who believe that forgiveness is just to good to be true. But notice the past-tense phrasing Paul used in Romans 6:1-7:

- "have died to sin"
- "were . . . buried with him"
- "old self was crucified"
- "has been set free"

The message of forgiveness is a message that deals with the past. By the past I mean what happened thirty years ago, twenty-five years ago, fifteen years ago, five years ago, five months ago, five days ago, and five minutes ago! The past has absolutely no more hold on the forgiven believer. The past has absolutely no bearing whatsoever on the manner in which God sees you now. When you come to the cross, forgiveness is given once and for all. Failed marriages, blown relationships, addictions, moral collapses, and abuses of many kinds—when placed at the feet of Jesus—are forgiven (1 John 1:7; Hebrews 9:12). And forgotten (Hebrews 8:12). That's his promise.

A powerful World War II story is told about a man named Simon Wiesenthal.[4] Wiesenthal, better known as the Nazi Hunter, spent most of his life tracking down war criminals associated with the Third Reich and, more specifically, with the atrocities committed in concentration camps throughout Europe.

On one occasion, Wiesenthal retold his experience of being taken from one of the death camps to an army hospital. Having no idea about the purpose of his journey, Wiesenthal hesitantly followed a nurse to the bedside of a fatally wounded Nazi soldier.

> When I meet someone who claims to be a Christ follower but possesses a casual attitude toward sin, I can't help wondering if a genuine conversion has taken place.

The soldier recounted the details of an unimaginable atrocity in which he had played a major role; he and his fellow comrades were the arsonists responsible for setting a Jewish village on fire. Men, women, and children died horrible, painful, and unnecessary deaths. His memory of the screams of the women and children had become too much for him to bear. The guilt, he felt, could only be remedied by forgiveness . . . from a Jew.

Wiesenthal desperately tried to leave the bedside of this unidentified soldier, but to no avail. The Nazi soldier, grabbing and holding on to his arm, began pleading with Wiesenthal to forgive—on behalf of all Jews—the sins he had committed. But Wiesenthal was unable to offer the forgiveness for which the soldier so desperately longed. He walked away. After all, Wiesenthal himself had lost eighty-nine of his own relatives at the hands of the Nazis and, at some point in his grief, had—according to certain sources—even attempted suicide.

Would you have offered forgiveness, had you been in Wiesenthal's place? Some time later fifty-three people would take the opportunity to respond to that question. These men and women were scholars, social theorists, psychologists, and others who were held in high regard in their respective fields. Their responses (published in a book called *The Sunflower*) reveal that the majority affirmed Wiesenthal's decision to withhold forgiveness, some saying he didn't have the right to offer that kind of forgiveness.

While it may be true that Wiesenthal did not have the right, or the power, to offer forgiveness on behalf of every Jewish person who had suffered because of this soldier, he did have the right to offer personal forgiveness for cruelty against himself. Had we been in his position, I'm sure we too would have had great difficulty in forgiving a man of such heinous crimes. But thankfully, God is not like us. No sin is too great that God cannot forgive a penitent heart.

King David stole another man's wife, got her pregnant, and then killed her husband to cover it all up (2 Samuel 11). Finally coming to his senses, David humbled himself before God, confessed his sins, and repented (12:13). Later in his life he would write, "As far as the east is from the west, so far has he removed our transgressions from us" (Psalm 103:12). Moreover, the apostle John, under the direction of the Holy Spirit, reminded the followers of Jesus that "if we confess our sins, he is faithful and just and will forgive us our sins and purify us from all unrighteousness" (1 John 1:9).

Forgiveness is so foreign to some people. The thought that God would forgive one's past sins, no matter how horrific, sounds simply too good to be true. I believe that God knew we would think this way. Perhaps that's why he highlights some "unforgivable" people in the Bible, even sets them up as our examples. How about Samson, Rahab, and Jonah?

> "I am writing to you, dear children, because your sins have been forgiven on account of his name."

He also chose a man whose past is far more atrocious than most of ours could ever be. Isn't it interesting that God chose someone responsible for the deaths of arguably hundreds of Christians to be the one who would launch the Christian movement in the Greco-Roman world? Think about it: Paul, the man responsible for writing most of the books in the New Testament, establishing the majority of churches in the first century, modeling the pattern for suffering to the first Christians, and recording the first thesis of theology and doctrine (the book of Romans) to some of the first believers, possessed a violent and alarming past.

Remember who Paul was before he was Paul? Saul, the lead persecutor of those who followed Jesus. Saul began his life of approving the killing of Christians when he was rather young. We're told that after Stephen preached the message of Christ, the Sanhedrin "covered their ears and, yelling at the top of their voices, they all rushed at him, dragged him out of the city and began to stone him. Meanwhile, the witnesses laid their coats at the feet of a young man named Saul. . . . And Saul approved of their killing him" (Acts 7:57, 58; 8:1).

So although no one knows with certainty, I often wonder whether God chose Paul just for those who believe that perhaps some sins are too great to be forgiven. If God can forgive genocide, he most definitely can forgive you. God promises to do so, and when God makes a promise, you can count on it. He communicates in his Word, "In [Jesus Christ] we have redemption through his blood, the forgiveness of sins, in accordance with the riches of God's grace" (Ephesians 1:7). And "I am writing to you, dear children, because your sins have been forgiven on account of his name" (1 John 2:12).

THOSE WHO HUMBLY EMBRACE FORGIVENESS

I remember seeing Lorraine Hansberry's play *A Raisin in the Sun*. It tells the story of a family in south Chicago in the 1950s struggling to keep their heads above water, looking and hoping for a better day. At a rather climactic point in the story, the father of the family passes away and leaves ten thousand dollars to his wife and children. The matriarch of the family believes that her dream of having a little house in Jersey will now become a reality. However, the son, seeing this as his only chance at a decent and respectable life, desperately begs for the money, promising the family that a business venture with a friend will yield an extravagant return. The mother doesn't want to do it; but as the son begs and pleads, her resolve is softened, and she gives in to her son's request, not wanting to deny him the opportunity.

Tragically, the young man's business partner takes the money and leaves town, stealing the only fortune the poor family from Harlem ever had. Beaten down, dreams destroyed, the young man returns home to break the news to his mother. His sister has no pity or compassion and rips into him like a tornado through a trailer park. With great consternation and contempt, she inquires as to his stupidity and tramples what little self-respect he may have had left.

After the encounter, the mother wonders aloud, "I thought I taught you to love him."

The sister replies, "There is nothing left to love."

But the mother says:

There is always something left to love. And if you ain't learned that, you ain't learned nothing. . . . Have you cried for that boy today? I don't mean for yourself and for the family 'cause we lost the money. I mean for him: what he been through and what it done to him. Child, when do you think is the time to love somebody the most? When they done good and made things easy for everybody? Well then, you ain't through learning—because that ain't the time at all. It's when he's at his lowest and can't believe in hisself 'cause the world done whipped him so! When you starts measuring somebody, measure him right, child, measure him right. Make sure you done taken into account what hills and valleys he come through before he got to wherever he is.[5]

Now there's a mother who understood forgiveness!

Those who follow Jesus are the sons and daughters of God. Our heavenly Father loves and cares for us like no other. And his greatest gift to us is the gift of forgiveness. Paul wrote to the church in Rome, "Blessed are those whose transgressions are forgiven, whose sins are covered" (Romans 4:7).

Why are those who have been forgiven so blessed? Forgiveness means that nothing stands between us and God. "If God is for us, who can be against us?" (8:31). Millions of people around the world have embraced God's forgiveness provided through the cross and now walk with their heads high, proud to call on the name of Jesus. There is something special about knowing who we truly are. Paul said that if he was going to boast in anything, he would boast in the cross (Galatians 6:14). For it is through this cross that forgiveness is ushered in and we become the beneficiaries of a benevolent God.

For many, the promise and gift of forgiveness is so overwhelming that they embrace it with weeping and gratitude. They realize that God reached out at a time when no one else would—when they were at their lowest because "the world done whipped them so!"—and offered the most precious gift of all: forgiveness.

WHICH PERSON **ARE YOU?**

So in which category do you find yourself? Have you rationalized your sin to the point where you honestly believe you have no need of forgiveness? But have you never had an impure thought, engaged in gossip or slander, violated a trust, uttered hurtful and harmful words, or willingly deceived someone? The Bible says that we are all sinners (Romans 3:23) in need of forgiveness. Perhaps this is the day when you will realize that your actions have wounded someone who has been created in the image of God. Maybe your eyes will be opened to the truth that all wrongdoing is an offense against a holy and just God who separates himself from sin. Perhaps today you will fess up to who you really are and what you have done, fall on your knees at the cross of Jesus Christ, find forgiveness, and begin to understand what it is like to live a life reconciled to God.

Do you see forgiveness as a license to do what you want to do without any ramifications? My father often warned my three brothers and me that God is not mocked, that "a man reaps what he sows" (Galatians 6:7). He believed that if you willingly and deliberately violate the law of God, God will withdraw his blessings from your life in that specific area. In other words, the Christ follower who moves in with his girlfriend to begin a new family says to God, "I am not going to obey you. I am going to do this my way. I do not want your involvement in my marriage and my family."

> For many, the promise and gift of forgiveness is so overwhelming that they embrace it with weeping and gratitude.

As a husband and father, I can tell you that in no other area of life do I long more for God's hand of blessing than with my marriage and children. How foolish, then, to mock God and expect him to open the windows of Heaven and rain down his blessings in the very area in which he has been scorned. Maybe today will be the day when you truly begin to see the law of God as something that is not arbitrarily given but, instead, comes to us from a loving Father who desires that his children experience the abundant life and who reserves the right to discipline his children when they deviate from the path of righteousness (Hebrews 12:6). Maybe today you will trust that your heavenly Father knows best and will begin to align your life with his will, thus positioning yourself to receive all the blessings that come with his promises.

Perhaps you fall into the third category. You have come to believe that the magnitude of your past sins is so great that God's promise to forgive no longer applies to you. My prayer for you is that the scales will be removed from your eyes and you will perhaps see the depth, height, and width of God's grace and forgiveness for the first time. In fact, all who have been instrumental in writing and editing this book deeply desire that through these pages you will experience a life-defining moment. A moment when it suddenly dawns on you that God's forgiveness is far greater than the worst of your sins.

Then you join the category of those who embrace forgiveness. God's promises are trustworthy. You and I may waver to the left and to the right, but the same God whose power creates and sustains such physical wonders as the sun, moon, and stars never turns away from his Word (James 1:17). He possesses the power and will to sustain every spiritual promise he has ever given. He has promised to forgive you. If you have never done so, repent and be baptized and receive the forgiveness of sins and the indwelling presence of the Holy Spirit (Acts 2:38). A new life can be yours. It's the life you have always wanted—set free from the past, placed into a glorious future, no longer separated from God but living fully in his presence, empowered to go where you have never gone before.

It's your move. God *promises* to forgive.

GREAT AND PRECIOUS PROMISES

FOR INDIVIDUAL OR GROUP STUDY

How have you reacted to God's forgiveness? Do you deny your need for it, do you abuse it, do you think it's too good to be true, or have you humbly received it?

1 If you deny a need for God's forgiveness, why? Like my college friend, do you think that you're basically a good person who occasionally does bad things? Why can't any one of us decide to just stop doing bad things?

2 Are you flirting with danger? Are you as far away from Jesus as you can be and still call yourself a Christian? The net of grace isn't there so you can jump on it anytime you like; it's there to catch you when you fall from the tightrope of holiness. If God sat across the table from you right now and had a conversation about your life, what areas do you think he would address? What would he have to say about your tightrope walking (or lack thereof)?

3 Do you feel that God's forgiveness is too good to be true? Why? Remember that Paul's past sins were atrocious, and yet God used him in many mighty ways. What is in your life that you feel God could never forgive? Ask him to forgive it, and he promises he will!

4 Have you humbly accepted the amazing forgiveness that God offers? How has your life changed as a result?

5 Think of someone from whom you've been withholding forgiveness. Was the offense "big" or "little"? Explain, if appropriate. How do you feel about your situation now that you've studied more about God's forgiveness? What will you do next?

CHAPTER SEVEN

I WILL
TRANSFORM YOU
JOHN 15:1-8

O NE OF THE MOST popular questions asked by major corporations is: How do we get from where we are to where we want to be? Let's say a company made $100,000 profit in the last fiscal year. This year they want to double their profit margin. How do they get from "here" to "there"? All leaders must ask this question if advancement or growth is their objective.

Once a person responds to Jesus' invitation of grace, mercy, and forgiveness, the most wonderful gift is given. The apostle Paul called this gift "the mystery that has been kept hidden for ages and generations, but is now disclosed to the Lord's people" (Colossians 1:26). What is the mystery? "Christ in you, the hope of glory" (v. 27). It is the reality of Jesus Christ living inside his people. The gift of his Spirit is God's solution to our failure to live a holy and pure life. While the cross removes our guilt, something must be done to move us from here (living as slaves to sin) to there (living free from sin's power).

The answer? God determined that all who would receive the gift of salvation would also receive the gift of the Holy Spirit (Acts 2:38). In other words, God gives us the promise of his presence in us in order that we might be transformed, day by day, into the people God wants us to become. He not only changes what we *do* but what we *want* to do.

GOOGLE EARTH: THE VIEW **FROM 40,000 FEET**
When I first discovered Google Earth, I sat at my computer late into the night,

looking for all the places I had lived. I began with a bird's-eye view of Number Seven Stoney Road in the suburb called Greencroft in the city of Harare, Zimbabwe, where my wife and I had lived as missionaries. I really think I saw a golf ball on top of our old house! I moused around the globe, looking for familiar identifying markers. For the most part my perspective was limited to the view from a few thousand feet. If I'd been trying to navigate using this method, my directions would have often been obscured by obstacles in my way or blurry paths.

> How can he possibly change my selfish desires,
> passions, hopes, and dreams into pure ones?

When Google Maps came out, any uncertainty in my mind concerning God's existence was removed. OK, just kidding. I have always believed in God; this was just another confirmation. When I first learned how to use Google Maps, I was pumped! Even though I am directionally challenged by nature, I found that by using Google Maps, I would never have to pull over and ask for directions again. I not only knew the general direction in which I was supposed to travel, but I also had detail!

Detail. That's what I am looking for.

I want to know in detail how God intends to transform me. How can he possibly change my selfish desires, passions, hopes, and dreams into pure ones? How can he give me the victory over all the temptations that come my way? How can he move me, as Paul put it, "from glory to glory" (2 Corinthians 3:18, *KJV*), from one level of growth to another level of growth?

When I was a student at Johnson Bible College (now Johnson University), those were questions I desperately wanted answered. I wanted to be transformed. I needed to be transformed. However, I did not yet understand the process of transformation—or the road map that clearly pointed out the manner in which God works to get me from here to there.

THE VINE AND **THE BRANCHES**

I know of no better description of the transforming work of the Holy Spirit than John 15:1-8. In this little section of Scripture, Jesus revealed the fact that transformation is a team effort. Without God, we would never start our journey, and if we hope to go where we have never been before, we have to be intentional about our growth. As we take a look at this passage, keep in mind that the purpose of the Holy Spirit in us is that we may become more like Christ. The fruit of the Spirit defines what Christlikeness looks like: "love, joy, peace, forbearance, kindness, goodness, faithfulness, gentleness and self-control" (Galatians 5:22). So how is such fruit, fruit that resembles Jesus' character, possible?

Jesus said, "I am the vine; you are the branches. If you remain in me and I in you, you will bear much fruit; apart from me you can do nothing" (John 15:5). Jesus described the believer's new life as a branch that is attached to the vine. That metaphor is powerful. A branch growing from a vine becomes the recipient of the life and nutrients that flow from the vine.

We often see agricultural illustrations used in the Bible to describe treasured truths. In addition to this discussion about the vine and the branches, the kingdom of God is also described as a mustard seed (Matthew 13:31, 32), and the sharing of the gospel is compared to sowing seed (Mark 4:1-20).

When good seed is planted in good soil, a plant takes root and begins to grow. Dirt gives rise to plants because of the seed planted. Dirt and plant life do not possess a great sense of mission—the ability to will and to do. Animals may have a greater sense of mission than plants, but their ability to act pales in comparison to a human being's ability. The human is able to process difficult information, have opinions about it, and act on it. Animals may experience the rudiments of feelings and emotions, but they do not grieve or rejoice in the same manner and to the same depths as do humans. Each order of life feels more deeply, acts more intentionally, and possesses a greater sense of awareness than the order of life just below it.

When Jesus promises to transform us, he is promising to live inside us. And as we submit to Jesus Christ and his Holy Spirit, we live on a higher order of living. We are attached to God—as branches to the vine—and his life flows into us. The impact is staggering.

- We are able to see things we had not previously seen.
- We are able to do things we never thought we could do.
- We are able to feel things we have never felt before.

A GREATER SENSE OF SEEING

Paul clearly states in 2 Corinthians 4:4 that "the god of this age has blinded the minds of unbelievers, so that they cannot see the light of the gospel that displays the glory of Christ, who is the image of God." It should come as no surprise to us that many of our nonbelieving friends seem to be unaware of the spiritual things that are now so clear to us. There is a reason for this: without God's Spirit living inside them, they have limited vision. They cannot view what God would like for them to see because they have not partnered with him to benefit from his enabling *power* to see.

While serving as a pastor in New Zealand, the managing director of Qantas Airlines became a member of our church. She began upgrading me to first class every time I flew to Los Angeles. It was a fantastic experience! Anytime I walked up the stairs to board, I was greeted by a man in a bow tie. He already knew my name and offered to get me whatever I wanted. I would usually order a steak, drink my favorite beverages, and then settle down to some coffee and chocolate.

After a while an interesting thing happened. I began to believe that I belonged. I remember on one occasion thinking about "those poor people" in economy. I did not really feel sorry for them; it was more of a smug arrogance that came over me. Suddenly, the Holy Spirit interrupted to remind me that I did not belong in first class but was there only because of the grace and mercy of someone who appreciated pastors and the work they do. God reminded me that my arrogance and prejudice were wrong and disappointing. I immediately repented.

> A branch growing from a vine becomes the recipient of the life and nutrients that flow from the vine.

Interestingly, I never received a first-class upgrade again. My friend at Qantas was transferred!

Without the governance of the Holy Spirit, that kind of unholy arrogance remains unchecked. When people do not view others through the lens of the Holy Spirit, self-centeredness takes over.

Think of some of the genocides of the twentieth century (for example, in Germany, Rwanda, Turkey, China, and Bosnia). These could not have occurred without the willingness of one group of people to see itself as superior to another. When pride and arrogance run rampant, the stage is set for marginalization, oppression, and dehumanization. With our typical desire for preeminence—and without the power of the Spirit to keep self-centeredness in check—people will gravitate toward philosophies that do indeed give rise to a sense of superiority and all the ramifications that ensue.

But those who have come to Christ have had their eyes opened and are able to see things others do not see—the danger of sin, the worth of every human being, the grace and mercy of God, and that an attitude of entitlement is self-serving.

Without Jesus, equality is hard to find. With Jesus, it's as Paul says: "Here there is no Gentile or Jew, circumcised or uncircumcised, barbarian, Scythian, slave or free, but Christ is all, and is in all. Therefore, as God's chosen people, holy and dearly loved, clothe yourselves with compassion, kindness, humility, gentleness and patience. Bear with each other and forgive one another if any of you has a grievance against someone. Forgive as the Lord forgave you. And over all these virtues put on love, which binds them all together in perfect unity" (Colossians 3:11-14). With Jesus, our hearts are transformed and our eyes opened to the essential worth and dignity of every person.

> "After I became a Christian, something just clicked inside me, telling me that I no longer had to be a slave to anything other than Christ."

When we are called to a higher order of living, we see what I call divine realities, things of greater importance that come into view now that Jesus lives in us.

As he was preparing for his death on the cross, Jesus warned his disciples that they wouldn't see him anymore. But for the follower of Christ, Jesus promised, "Before long, the world will not see me anymore, but you will see me. Because I live, you also will live" (John 14:19). The sight Jesus brings is a different kind of seeing, just as the life he gives is a different kind of living.

A GREATER SENSE OF DOING

Not only are we able to see things we have never seen; we are also able to do things we previously could not do. Thomas Chalmers (1780–1847), a minister in Scotland, referred to the work of the Holy Spirit as "the expulsive power of a new affection."[1] No longer slaves to sin, we who have Christ in us possess the power to say no to sin. So Paul instructs us: "Do not let sin reign in your mortal body so that you obey its evil desires. Do not offer any part of yourself to sin as an instrument of wickedness, but rather offer yourselves to God as those who have been brought from death to life; and offer every part of yourself to him as an instrument of righteousness" (Romans 6:12, 13).

While serving at one church, I became close friends with a recovering alcoholic. Jack (not his real name) was an extremely talented sportsman. We shared a passion for golf and enjoyed a couple of rounds a month. During one of our rounds, I asked Jack how he had managed to stay sober for more than twenty years. He said, "After I became a Christian, something just clicked inside me, telling me that I no longer had to be a slave to anything other than Christ. I stopped drinking immediately when I realized 'I can do all this through him who gives me strength'" (Philippians 4:13).

Likewise, a young pastor who asked me to mentor him had struggled with pornography early in his ministry. I asked how he managed to free himself from the shackles. His response is classic: "One day I was reading Romans 6:12, 13, where Paul, under the inspiration of the Holy Spirit, commands us to stop giving sin permission to use the members of our body to quench its unholy appetites. So I figured that if we were powerless against sin, well, Paul would not have pretended that we weren't. So now, when sin asks to use my eyes to look at something I should not, I just say no."

Simplistic? Yes, unless a person realizes that he is connected to the vine. Jesus is the source of our ability to overcome the most intense temptations and hardships. The apostle Paul also said, "[The Lord] said to me, 'My grace is sufficient for you, for my power is made perfect in weakness.' Therefore I will boast all the more gladly about my weaknesses, so that Christ's power may rest on me" (2 Corinthians 12:9). It is the Holy Spirit's strength that can help us do what we think we cannot.

A GREATER SENSE OF FEELING

The Holy Spirit, the new life in our new lives, enables us to see things we have never seen, do things we have never done, and feel things we have never felt. For many Christians, *feeling* one's faith is a top priority. "I don't feel God's presence. Why don't I feel my faith?" is perhaps the most desperate question we hear in our church office. I believe we have forgotten that our ability to *do* and our ability to *feel* are closely related.

Moses learned this valuable lesson. Apprehensive about his calling and uncertain that God would give him what he needed to lead the children of Israel into the promised land, Moses requested a sign. God's response shows the relationship between obedience and feeling. God said, "I will be with you. And this will be the sign to you that it is I who have sent you: When you have brought the people out of Egypt, you will worship God on this mountain" (Exodus 3:12).

Fascinating, isn't it? If Moses wanted to feel the presence of God, he had to first do what God had called him to do. Obedience and "feeling my faith" are inextricably tied together. In fact, I believe that to some extent we have lost our ability to feel God's presence because we have lost our willingness to obey him. If we want to feel God's presence in our lives, we must listen to and heed his Word. For instance, if God's Word indicates that I should do something really difficult—break off that relationship, leave that job, sever ties with that business partner, forgive that family member, or forsake that recreation—and I refuse, it makes perfect sense that over time, as things don't go well, I will begin to feel as though God has removed himself from me and my situation.

However, when the Spirit of God calls me to obey him in a very difficult situation, and I respond with absolute allegiance to the Word of God, after I come out on the other side of the fire victoriously, I will feel like Moses on the mountaintop—full of worship and appreciation for the comfort and strength I received from the God who "came near" when I needed him most.

Notice then, feeling God's presence requires obedience. And obeying God requires an acute awareness of his Word and his expectations. And becoming aware of his Word and expectations requires a transformational overhaul from inside out.

Those who have been called to a higher order of living as a result of God's Spirit living in them possess a greater sense of awareness (that's the "seeing") and a greater sense of mission (that's the "doing"), which in turn leads to a greater ability to feel the presence of God in their lives. If you want to feel God in a way you never have before, then obey the promptings of the Spirit. And you, like Moses, will stand on the mountain and worship him.

TRANSFORMING INTO **CHRISTLIKENESS**

Once we are grafted into the vine, we are nourished by the Father, Son, and Holy Spirit. We see, do, and feel things we have never seen, done, or felt before. This is the result of the power of new life dwelling in us. The question now is this: As branches on the vine, how do we begin to bear more and more fruit as each day goes by? How can we make sure that we are always moving forward, growing more and more like Christ? This is precisely the question Jesus answered in John 15:5 when he reminded the disciples that they must remain in him, saying, "Apart from me you can do nothing."

I believe this was a catalytic moment in Jesus' relationship with his disciples. Aware that the day was soon approaching when he would no longer be with them (at least in the flesh), Jesus gave clear direction concerning the manner in which the life he was calling them to live could be actualized. He began with a simple reminder concerning the origin of holiness.

Who is the vine? Jesus.

Who are the branches? Believers.

That's easy enough, but the next question requires a bit more contemplation. Do we *produce* fruit or *bear* fruit? It's a question of origin. What is the source that produces spiritual fruit in us? Christ. As long as we stay attached to the vine, bearing fruit will be the natural result.

We cannot produce (that is, create) fruit on our own. God initiates the growth; and when we cooperate with him, fruit will naturally appear. Without the vine, no nutrients flow into our lives. We must remain connected to the life source. Then and only then will we bear much fruit. How do we remain connected to the vine so that we may bear spiritual fruit? In John 15:7 Jesus said, "If you remain in me and my words remain in you, ask whatever you wish, and it will be done for you."

> I believe that to some extent we have lost our ability to feel God's presence because we have lost our willingness to obey him.

Was Jesus claiming to be the genie in the bottle? Just ask him for anything you want and it will be yours? A Mercedes, a beach house, a million dollars, or anything else? Of course not. The context is in relation to the fruit of the Spirit. Jesus was saying that if it's spiritual growth you really want, then ask for it (joy, peace, kindness, self-control, and so forth). God will unleash his life-sustaining power into your life and place you in situations (sometimes difficult ones) until you transform into something you never thought you could become. The only requirement is that you must remain in his words and his words must remain in you.

WHAT DOES THAT **LOOK LIKE?**

When Nelson Mandela became the president of South Africa, he decided that the best way to heal his torn country after apartheid was through reconciliation. This was amazingly brave. Most African leaders were calling for retribution. Instead of going in that direction, Mandela established what became known as South Africa's Truth and Reconciliation Commission (TRC).[2]

Courtrooms were set up throughout South Africa in which whites in positions of authority were given the chance to confess their crimes in full to those they had offended. If full disclosure was given and genuine remorse shown, there was the possibility that no prison time would be required and reconciliation could occur.

> In order that she might win the victory over the temptation to hate and exact revenge, she had filled her mind with the Word of God.

While living in New Zealand, I heard an amazing story about one of these TRC hearings. A black woman entered the courtroom with a group of supporters behind her. As a young, white policeman took the stand, the courtroom grew quiet. Finally, the woman, aware of this policeman's role in the death of her husband and sixteen-year-old son, confronted the officer with two questions. She first inquired as to the circumstances surrounding the death of the two people she dearly loved. Then she asked about the whereabouts of her husband's and son's remains.

Visibly disturbed and showing great remorse, the officer began to share how he and a few other officers had found the husband in a restricted area and murdered him in a brutal, torturous way. Then just a few weeks later, finding her young son out past curfew, the officers repeated the same dastardly deed before burying what was left of the body.

After a few moments of silence in the courtroom, the woman began to speak. She told the court that she had two requests for the officer. She first asked the officer—whose head was bowed low, embarrassed and shamed by his role in the horrendous affair—to take her to the place where her husband and son were buried.

This came as no surprise to anyone in the courtroom. A proper burial for loved ones is very important in the woman's culture. However, what followed next stunned the crowd and humbled the officer. The woman (a Christian), with tears in her eyes, spoke of how she still had a lot of love to give but no son or husband to give it to. Therefore, she requested that the young policeman visit her home every week so that she could cook him a meal and give this love in her heart to him. When the young officer heard this request, he was so overwhelmed by the measure of forgiveness that he wept loudly. Suddenly, the small support group attending the hearing stood and broke into a chorus of "Amazing Grace."

I tell this remarkable story because of something else that occurred in regard to this event. During my annual trip to Zimbabwe and Rwanda, I met Nicholas, a journalist who actually had sat in the courtroom in South Africa that day. He told me that when the woman was asked how she was able to give such grace and forgiveness in the midst of such a horrible offense, her response was eye-opening. She spoke of saturating her mind with the words of Jesus: "If you forgive other people when they sin against you, your heavenly Father will also forgive you" (Matthew 6:14). She spoke of human nature, the power of the flesh, and how she knew that when she walked into the courtroom, the flesh, left unchecked, would take over and walk her toward retribution, not reconciliation.

Therefore, in order that she might win the victory over the temptation to hate and exact revenge, she had filled her mind with the Word of God so that when the time came, she could grab her emotions by the scruff of the neck and lead them to the truth—that if we forgive others, God will forgive us.

When I heard Nicholas recount that episode, I was reminded once again of those seasons in my life when I seemed to have transformed into a new person. Looking back, I am able to see a common denominator that was present during times of growth: daily reading and meditation on the Word of God.

Romans 12:2 warns us, "Do not conform to the pattern of this world, but be transformed by the renewing of your mind. Then you will be able to test and approve what God's will is—his good, pleasing and perfect will." Without the daily discipline of saturating our minds with the Word of God, the *words* of God do not remain in us, and the ramifications are tragic.

The evil one exists (1 John 5:19). God's Word is our ammunition against him. That's why Paul said, "Put on the full armor of God, so that you can take your stand against the devil's schemes. . . . Take up the shield of faith, with which you can extinguish all the flaming arrows of the evil one. Take . . . the sword of the Spirit, which is the word of God" (Ephesians 6:11, 16, 17). We are bombarded daily by philosophies and temptations that are contrary to the way of Christ. When the words of God are not in us, we have no ammunition. Remaining in the Word and making sure the Word remains in us is not only vital to our growth—it is critical to our survival!

That kind of "remaining," or abiding, allows the Holy Spirit to give us the right word at the right time at the right place to secure victory over the psychological, physical, emotional, and spiritual battles of our lives. When we are so saturated with and governed by the Word of God, our actions will confirm that we are his disciples (John 15:8).

It's a partnership of transformation. When we accept Christ, we receive the Spirit; and as we continue to read the Word of God, the Spirit speaks to us through the God-breathed words and uses these words to transform our thinking and, as a result, our actions. How does this work itself out pragmatically in our everyday situations? For example:

- Family tension is about to erupt over whose home will be the location of this year's Christmas gathering. You're sure that you gave in last year to the wishes of others; it's your turn to have your way this time. Then you recall: "If it is possible, as far as it depends on you, live at peace with everyone" (Romans 12:18).

- The boss is on your case—again (and you don't even see yourself as the cause of his complaint). You're ready to lash back . . . but then recall: "A gentle answer turns away wrath, but a harsh word stirs up anger" (Proverbs 15:1).

- You've taken a stand. It was the right thing to do. Now it's the middle of the night and you're pacing the floor, worried about the repercussions. Joshua 1:9 comes to mind: "Do not be afraid; do not be discouraged, for the LORD your God will be with you."

- As a young business executive, you're about to be carried away by thoughts of great wealth and a life of materialistic pursuits. The Spirit activates Christ's words: "No one can serve two masters. Either you will hate the one and love the other, or you will be devoted to the one and despise the other. You cannot serve both God and money" (Matthew 6:24). Your eyes are opened, and you repent of your greed.

When you abide in the vine, the Spirit of God can transform you. Even our deepest, most debilitating psychological and emotional illnesses can be overcome by the power of Christ in us. I have been transparent with my congregation concerning my struggle with depression. Depression is an incredibly debilitating disease and one the medical world cannot quite figure out. Over the years, however, I have learned the most wonderful truth: we cannot always trust our emotions!

> Within a few minutes I was singing in my car,
> waving my hands, and worshipping!

Like most people who struggle with depression, I find that devastating events in my life tend to trigger the spiraling down of emotions. When my mom died, it was one of the most difficult times of my life. I did the only thing I knew to do: go to the Bible for answers and pray that God would speak. I just kept filling my mind with the Word of God, especially the passages that address losing those we love.

About three months had passed when I was driving back from a speaking trip some three hours north of Auckland, New Zealand. Suddenly, I glanced toward an exit ramp off Highway 1 and noticed it read, "Dargaville." I remembered this as the spot where just a few months earlier I'd received the phone call from my brother informing me that my mother was fighting for her life. Recalling those events immediately started the downward spiral. Then it was as if the Spirit of God said, "The one who believes in me will live, even though they die" (John 11:25). Those words came into my mind over and over again.

Within a few minutes I was singing, waving my hands, and worshipping! I kept thinking of my mom up in Heaven, dancing and rejoicing with Jesus, with no pain, sorrow, or suffering—having the time of her life! God kept reminding me of all the Scripture I had read over the last three months. When I read it then, I did not necessarily see all the relevance, but when the time came—because I am attached to the vine and was remaining in his Word—he gave me the right words. "He lifted me . . . out of the mud and mire; he set my feet on a rock" (Psalm 40:2). He showed me the way to victory!

If we saturate our minds with the Word—*and* develop the art of getting out of the way so the Spirit can activate the right word at the right time!—we can live above those circumstances that would reduce our spiritual and emotional vitality.

FROM HERE **TO THERE**

We began this chapter by describing that it is difficult to move from "here" to "there" without great intentionality. The "here" for Christ followers can be, unfortunately, a life that seems stagnant with very little significant growth. After twenty-six years of ministry, I have come to realize that in many cases, the reason has more to do with a lack of knowledge than a lack of passion. We *want* to bear fruit but are uninformed concerning the fruit-bearing basics. Consequently, the "there," the place where life is filled with the fruit of the Spirit, remains unrealized.

I find myself wishing I had a Google Maps translation of the Bible—ten, one-line, clear, orderly steps to reach one's destination. Yet upon closer investigation, I am reminded that though the steps may not be numbered in the Bible, the message *is* clear. To move from here (spiritual stagnation) to there (spiritual productivity), to be transformed, we must remember to do a few things:

1. Recognize the divine source that makes fruit-bearing possible.
2. Stay close to the source by saturating our minds with his Word.
3. Wait for the Holy Spirit to activate the right word at the right time.
4. Obey the word that the Spirit brings to mind.
5. Acknowledge the fruit that is born as a result of our obedience.

Nowhere have I seen this dynamic played out more powerfully than in the life of my friend Anna. Anna always felt she could never live up to her father's expectations. As a result, there was very little joy in her life. At age sixteen she left home, searching for someone who would give her the unconditional love and acceptance she desperately longed for.

Unfortunately, she met a man who was nothing more than a younger version of her father. Then she turned to a church. Sadly, this church presented God as nothing more than a glorified version of her father, a God whose love and acceptance were based solely on effort and performance. Feeling once again that she could never measure up, she left everything and everyone and moved overseas. When I met Anna, she had been searching for love and acceptance for almost twenty years and, in fact, had come close to ruining her life by engaging in highly questionable activities in her attempts to reach her goal.

When I shared the gospel of grace with her, she wept. When a person discovers that God's genuine love and acceptance are not based on what we do, but on what Jesus *did* two thousand years ago on the cross, the indescribable joy is overwhelming. An even greater passion for holiness results—not out of an attempt to earn God's favor, but out of an appreciation for the unmerited favor already given through the cross.

But old habits die hard. There are times when the old Anna creeps back in. Seasons come when she feels that she is not good enough to be a Christ follower, when even a relatively small moral failure convinces her that she has forfeited her right to be called a child of God. Immediately, her joy dissipates and she finds it difficult to find her way home. But she does—every single time!

How does she do that?

1. She reminds herself that joy is a spiritual gift that comes from staying close to Jesus. So she becomes more disciplined in her time alone in meditation and prayer.
2. She saturates her mind with the Word of God, placing key Bible verses on her desk at work and on her refrigerator door at home. Verses like Romans 8:1, "There is now no condemnation for those who are in Christ Jesus," and Romans 5:1, "Since we have been justified through faith, we have peace with God through our Lord Jesus Christ," and Ephesians 2:8, 9, which states, "It is by grace you have been saved, through faith—and this is not from yourselves, it is the gift of God—not by works, so that no one can boast."
3. When she feels herself slipping into depression, she gives space for the Holy Spirit to activate the words of truth.
4. Then she forces herself to submit to the truth.
5. She sees—and is amazed at—the fruit the Spirit is gradually producing in her. Rather than joy being the exception, it has now become the rule. She says, "I am known around the office as Happy Anna."

It is amazing what intentionality can do. Anna has moved from here to there, she is being transformed, through purposefully remaining close to Jesus and allowing Jesus' words to remain close to her.

Where is your "here"? Does it seem like the "there" you want to reach is far away? No matter where you are now in your journey of faith, if you remain close to Jesus, you can be transformed too. It's a promise.

GREAT AND PRECIOUS PROMISES

FOR INDIVIDUAL OR GROUP STUDY

God gives us direct access to the power that transforms, but as with the gift of salvation, we must reach out and take hold of the gift God has offered. In the same way he does not force his salvation on us, neither does he force sanctification (or, becoming more like him). Unlike a branch, which has no choice in whether it stays on a vine or gets cut off, we have a choice. We can choose to follow the path to sanctification, the path to growth. Jesus is clear concerning how that happens: we remain in his words and his words remain in us. God's will for our lives includes both salvation and sanctification. He not only desires to save us from our sins but also to transform us.

1 In what specific ways have you seen progression toward Christlikeness over the course of your life since you became a Christian? Can you identify seasons of real growth? seasons of stagnation? Can you identify the difference between those two kinds of seasons? Why do you think those seasons occur?

2 What are some of the ways in which the Holy Spirit has impacted the things you see, do, and feel?

3 There is a direct correlation between obeying God and feeling his presence. If you feel far from God, take the time right now to pray and confess those areas in which you have been disobedient to him. How can you obey him now so that you will soon be able to feel his presence again?

4 What's the difference between producing fruit and bearing fruit? How can you get on board with what God wants to do in your life?

There must be ammunition with which to fight the evil one. In what practical ways are you currently saturating your mind with the Word of God? What are some favorite verses that you have recently committed to memory?

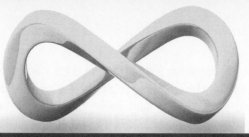

CHAPTER EIGHT

I WILL
GIVE YOU SPIRITUAL GIFTS
ROMANS 12:3-8

WHEN JESUS CALLED PETER, Andrew, James, and John to be his disciples, something quite amazing happened. To these four men, fishing was a way of life. Fishing was what they did; it was who they were. It's possible that they spent little time thinking of anything else—until they had an encounter with a carpenter from Nazareth.

When Peter met Jesus, he and his brother Andrew had been fishing all night and had caught nothing. (Not a good way to stay ahead of your competitors.) Then Jesus commandeered their boat as a makeshift pulpit. Although we really have no idea what Jesus taught that day, his words obviously challenged Peter to consider what he was doing with his life.

After teaching, Jesus commanded Peter to sail out into deep water and drop the nets. Peter did so with a noticeable measure of reluctance. Suddenly, however, the tug on the nets must have been overpowering, because Peter had to get all hands on deck to reel in the catch. Recognizing that this large catch had nothing to do with his fishing skills and everything to do with the power of Jesus, Peter humbly pleaded, "Go away from me, Lord; I am a sinful man!" (Luke 5:1-8).

But Jesus had other intentions; he offered an amazing, life-defining invitation: "Come, follow me, and I will send you out to fish for people" (Matthew 4:19).

The manner in which Jesus phrased his call to these four fishermen is intriguing. Jesus invited them to use their "reeling in" skills for the sake of eternity—to bring those far from God into the boat of God's kingdom; to go out into deep waters where people were drowning under the weight of guilt and sin, and gather them into the net of God's grace, mercy, and forgiveness.

What was going on in the minds of these four men before this event? Were they satisfied with their lives, or had they been thinking, *There's got to be something more?* One thing is certain: when they heard Jesus' invitation, they immediately left their nets and followed him—though they couldn't have known the far-reaching impact their decision would have.

THE GIFT OF THE **HOLY SPIRIT**

Upon hearing and accepting the good news of the gospel, a person receives the gift of the Holy Spirit. This is the presence of God indwelling the believer for the purpose of conforming him or her to be more like Christ.

Successful transformation from who we are to who Christ calls us to be requires two separate actions. God does his part by placing his Spirit in us to guide and direct us toward paths of righteousness. However, we must choose to walk those paths. This is why Paul urged the Roman Christians to "be transformed by the renewing of your mind" (Romans 12:2). In other words, we must saturate our minds with God's Word and then respond when the Spirit's conviction comes. That's the biblical recipe for transformation (as we studied in chapter 7).

> God does his part by placing his Spirit in us to guide and direct us toward paths of righteousness.

Part of the Holy Spirit's work is to initiate spiritual gifts in the life of the believer. In fact, in Romans 12:1 Paul challenged believers to "offer your bodies as a living sacrifice, holy and pleasing to God—this is your true and proper worship." To worship the living God, we must submit our gifts, talents, abilities, and yes, even our very own bodies, to the lordship of Christ.

"The will of God, concerning which Paul has just spoken [*in Romans 12:1, 2*], is identical for all believers in respect to holiness of life and completeness of dedication. But what that will involves for each one with respect to special service in the church may be considerably diverse."[1]

SPIRITUAL GIFTS 101

The apostle Paul told the believers in Corinth that he did not want them "to be uninformed" about the gifts of the Spirit (1 Corinthians 12:1). A spiritual gift is an unmerited, unearned talent given by God for the purpose of building his kingdom on the earth. Spiritual gifts are just that—gifts. Any pride associated with spiritual gifts is nonsensical. This was Paul's point when he warned believers: "Do not think of yourself more highly than you ought, but rather think of yourself with sober judgment, in accordance with the faith God has distributed to each of you" (Romans 12:3). God is the author and distributor of the gifts. Be grateful, not prideful.

> These unlearned men became preachers,
> teachers, and writers who changed the world!

Sometimes the Holy Spirit brings a sort of supernatural injection to talents and abilities you were born with. In other words, you may have a natural gift of music, teaching, leading, or helping; but when you submit that gift to Christ and his kingdom, he blesses that gift and transforms it into something greater, spiritually speaking.

However, there are times when God gives a believer a brand-new gift that has very little to do with what that person was before coming to Christ. God may take a person who is a timid public speaker and inject that person with a gift that suddenly enables him to write and deliver inspiring speeches. Think about Peter, Andrew, James, and John again. They may have possessed entrepreneurial skills to grow a business; but typically, fishermen were not among the educated. Yet these unlearned men became preachers, teachers, and writers who changed the world! The Holy Spirit not only supercharged their existing talents and abilities; he also equipped them with brand-new gifts.

Why does God give these gifts? Hebrews 2:4 says that God confirms the salvation he offers people "by signs, wonders and various miracles, and by gifts of the Holy Spirit distributed according to his will." God loves his church and wants to see every group of believers effectively take the gospel message into the community, so he offers a diverse collection of gifts and talents that will allow us to do that. After all, he created the tremendous diversity of personality types we find in this world. What motivates, communicates to, or resonates with one group of people leaves an entirely different group of people unmoved, unmotivated, and unchanged.

Simply put, it takes all kinds. I believe that God gave different gifts, in part, to reach different types of people. Think of a chessboard: each piece on the board plays a unique role to achieve the same objective—the winning of the game. So it is with the church of the living God. Each of us plays a unique, important role in a larger eternal mission—our gifts help and grow the local church, which helps and expands Christ's kingdom in the world.

I firmly believe that if you are regularly attending church and have settled into a church home, then your participation in that church is no accident. I believe in a sovereign God who moves the pieces of the chessboard from one place to another to accomplish his purposes. God called you to your church because there was a hole that only you, with your unique set of talents, abilities, and gifting, could fill.

LEARN TO SWIM (AKA DISCOVER YOUR GIFTS)

Though we're probably more likely to be overly *proud* of our talents and accomplishments, some people say, "I don't have any talents" or "I'm not good at anything." But Jesus counteracts that with these words: "Whoever believes in me will do the works I have been doing, and they will do even greater things than these" (John 14:12). Did you catch that? If you are a follower of Jesus, there must be something you have been equipped to do. What is it?

I did not learn to swim until I was seventeen years old. My mom and dad were terrified of water and never let me go near it. All that changed one day when I met a girl whose forte was swimming and whose passion was deep water. There was no way I was going to let this girl know that I couldn't swim.

My buddies took me to the pool to teach me the art of staying afloat. Unfortunately—or fortunately, depending on how you look at it—they believed that the most expedient way to teach me to swim was to throw me into the deep end. My friends pushed me in, and after a couple of seconds kicking, screaming, and fighting for my life, I just started kicking my feet and flapping my arms, and somehow I didn't sink. OK, so I was not necessarily swimming yet, but it was a start.

Discovering and using your spiritual gifts is often similar to learning to swim. One option is to take weeks and weeks of swimming lessons to prepare for the big day when you can swim in the deep end. Another way is to simply jump in (or have friends push)! My personal opinion is that there's a place for both options.

If you wait until you know exactly how God has gifted you and where you are meant to serve, many opportunities may pass you by. Instead, jump in! Just start serving where you are desperately needed. At the same time, you can be asking the right questions, methodically and carefully, on your journey to discover your primary gifts. Let's look at a few of the spiritual gifts that God promised to give to his followers.

PROPHECY

The Greek word for prophecy is *propheteia,* which means "admonishing the wicked" or "comforting the afflicted."[2] In the New Testament, prophecy was not typically a foretelling of future events but was simply proclaiming the truth of Jesus and urging the congregation to follow the teachings of Jesus. First Corinthians 14:1 emphasizes the importance of this gift: "Eagerly desire gifts of the Spirit, especially prophecy."

Some people have the uncanny ability to encourage and motivate others to follow the ways of Christ. They do so with intense passion and amazing clarity. So if you like to stand up in front of people and tell them what to do, you might have this gift!

First Corinthians 14:3 says, "One who prophesies speaks to people for their strengthening, encouraging and comfort." And Romans 12:6 says, "If your gift is prophesying, then prophesy in accordance with your faith" (or "according to the proportion of faith," *KJV*). One who has this gift builds up, equips, challenges, and encourages. However, Paul clearly indicates that there are different measures of the same gift. In other words, some may be equipped to prophesy to hundreds; others, to thousands; and some, just to tens. Or the kinds of messages delivered may differ. There are people gifted at simple, cut-to-the-chase messages while others can expound on complex issues of life and faith. Or the gift of prophecy may be given with a particular audience in mind.

SERVICE

Romans 12:7 says, "If it is serving, then serve." The gift of service, or ministry, is also called the gift of helps. People who serve jump in and get the job done—they don't sit around talking about or listening to what should be done. These godly servants never say, "That's not my job." They are energized by the fact that something needs to be done, and they are the ones to do it!

I can illustrate these above-and-beyond types of people by describing something I see at my favorite café. Like a lot of other pastors, I begin each morning with a cup of coffee. For more than two years, I've watched a particular waitress not only make coffee but go out of her way to serve the patrons who frequent this mom-and-pop shop. She makes more than cappuccinos; she makes art! Every morning she designs a little dragon or flower or some other work of art out of the foam covering my two shots of caffeine. And she does this for every customer while keeping everything spotless . . . and making minimum wage.

Now here is the beginning of the story: The people at Christ's Church of the Valley had been challenged to identify one person with whom they come into constant contact, and for whom they could begin to pray for God to orchestrate events toward helping the person cross over into a relationship with Jesus. This waitress became the person I prayed for.

Eventually, she gave her life to Christ. What happened next was predictable. With the Holy Spirit, her natural gifts of hospitality and service looked as if they had gone on steroids! She also became part of our welcoming ministry at church and began making cappuccinos and lattés for our guests, serving them with such passion that many first-timers felt so overwhelmed with love, they returned to our church hoping to see "Java Jana" again.

> If you wait until you know exactly how God has gifted you and where you are meant to serve, many opportunities may pass you by.

What may seem a menial task may in fact be a supernatural job with supernatural possibilities. The point is, if a person comes into a relationship with Jesus and already possesses a natural bent toward a specific service, the Holy Spirit will enhance that gift and lead the person into a variety of creative ways to use it.

For the first seven years of our church plant in New Zealand, we had to set up hundreds of chairs every Sunday morning. Volunteers would come in around 6:00 a.m. to begin the tedious task. One young man headed this ministry that entire seven years. That's a lot of work! He said he was doing his part, however small, in hopes that someone's life would be changed for God's glory. Pastors dream of guys like this! They are the glue that holds things together—dependable, generous servants who jump in and make things happen.

While not all people have this gift of service, all members of God's church are told to engage in serving others:

- "Encourage the disheartened, help the weak" (1 Thessalonians 5:14).
- "Serve one another humbly in love" (Galatians 5:13).
- "Do good to all people, especially . . . believers" (Galatians 6:10).
- "Carry each other's burdens" (Galatians 6:2).
- "[Look] . . . to the interests of the others" (Philippians 2:4).

Some people may not discover their spiritual gifts until they participate in various forms of simple service—finding a need that exists and stepping in to meet it. Often through the process of elimination, you will discover your true gifting.

TEACHING

Romans 12:7 says, "If it is teaching, then teach." The gift of teaching is the ability to categorize, systematize, and explain God's truth in a way that makes sense to others and promotes life change. (By the way, it's a safe bet that the people responsible for writing the instruction manuals for putting together a bicycle do not have this gift!)

> Maybe your experiences together with your teaching gift enable you to communicate to the next generation in a way that others cannot.

The Holy Spirit may give the gift of teaching to someone who previously did not seem to have it (like Peter, James, and John), but also may supercharge the gift when it's already present (as with Paul).

You may be gifted to teach a large audience in a clear and precise fashion. Or you may be great in small groups or one-on-one or with a particular age group.

It's amazing how God gifts teachers so that all the age groups in the church are covered. You might hear one person say, "I've been teaching the college class for ten years and never get tired of it," while another says, "I wouldn't know where to begin with college students!" Or one person says, "I just love teaching the five-year-olds," while another says, "I teach the adults. I'm not smart enough to teach little kids!"

Can you explain difficult concepts to teenagers? Teenagers are bombarded with lies: nothing is sacred; nothing is absolutely true; and God, faith, and Heaven are fabrications of the intellectually weak. If you have the gift of teaching teens, perhaps the struggles our teenagers face resonate with you because you remember the volatility and uncertainty of your own difficult teenage years. Maybe your experiences together with your teaching gift enable you to communicate to the next generation in a way that others cannot.

I have a gift of teaching; however, God gave this gift to me with some limitations. Junior highers sometimes try to stump me with a difficult question, like "Who made God?" I have a good answer—for seasoned apologists. Not so good for junior highers. But our children's pastor is able to respond to such questions with creative answers that even a child can understand. Same gift, different measure.

ENCOURAGING

Romans 12:8 says, "If it is to encourage, then give encouragement." The Greek word is *parakaleo,* meaning "to encourage and strengthen," "to comfort."[3] Years ago a man in my church would come into my office from time to time and say, "I got my eyes on you, Vines. How are you doing? I'm here for you." It's like he had a supernatural ability to say the right thing at the right time to encourage me. By the time he left my office, I felt I could conquer the world.

One of the most successful ministries in our church is Celebrate Recovery. One of our leaders determined to gather together our members who exhibited the gift of encouragement. The ripple effect has been staggering. This leader created an army of life coaches who come alongside those who are struggling with, as he calls it, "hurts, habits, and hang-ups." With no judgmental attitude, these men and women regularly meet and encourage those who are dealing with everything from addictions to relational wounds. The healing that is happening in our church right now has brought about a revival of prayer and worship and thanksgiving.

When Christians say they're waiting for God to "send revival to our churches," I say that God is waiting on *us*! When we all use our gifts to build up the body of Christ, revival will come! Even the use of a "little" gift like encouragement can bring big results.

GIVING

Romans 12:8 says, "If it is giving, then give generously." Though anyone *can* give, some people have the gift of giving—and not just financially but in many areas of life. They see all of life from an eternal perspective and thus understand that you can't take anything out of this world into the next. Therefore, they try to give away as much money, resources, and time as they can.

My friend Mike is perhaps the most generous man I know. Seven years ago he started ISOTECH Pest Management Inc., and has watched the company explode with growth and vitality. Every time I mention a well we need to dig in Africa or a pastor we need to support in India, Mike's eyes light up with the possibilities. He does not seem to be able to out-give God. The more generous he is with his money, the more willing God seems to be to give him more.

Unfortunately, not everyone sees generosity in this light. Once after I had spoken on the topic of stewardship, a lady came up to me and said, "Thank you, pastor, for clearing something up for me."

I responded, "What exactly did I clear up?"

She said, "I now know why I don't give. I don't have the gift."

Wait just a minute! We don't do *only* the thing we're gifted in. One may not have the gift of teaching, but all Christian fathers are commanded to bring up their children "in the training and instruction of the Lord" (Ephesians 6:4). One may not have the gift of service, but we are all told to follow Christ's example by humbling ourselves and serving one another (Philippians 2:5-8). Just because I do not have the gift of giving does not exempt me from giving my time, talents, and money to a purpose greater than myself. In fact, all of us will be held accountable for the way we used the resources God entrusted us with. The parable of the talents (Matthew 25:14-30) illustrates that accountability. Some of us just have a far easier time giving to God what originally came from him in the first place.

LEADERSHIP

Romans 12:8 says, "If it is to lead, do it diligently." A leader steers the ship, taking charge and guiding in a specific direction.

Having been a missionary for twenty years, I tend to have an international focus. But the elders at my church opened my eyes to how many hurting people are in our own community. I knew something had to be done. I recruited a few men and women I suspected of having a leadership gift, and they spearheaded food drives and clothing drives and ministries for moms in need. They took charge, guided, and got the job done. People with this gift not only see the need but also understand how the need can be met and, furthermore, how to motivate others to get on board.

The leadership gift, like all other gifts, is given in measure. Some may not be able to lead an entire church but are able to lead one particular ministry area. Some are called to lead huge projects on a regular basis, and others may only lead one specific initiative for a short time. Many kinds of leadership are necessary.

MERCY

Romans 12:8 says, "If it is to show mercy, do it cheerfully." The Greek word for "show mercy" is *eleeo,* meaning "to help one afflicted."[4] Showing mercy includes more than just giving words of encouragement. The mercy gift involves having enough compassion to actually put your hands to work and do something about it. The finest example I have ever seen of this gift came from Kyle and Bonnie Harrison, the Tennessee farm couple with whom my wife and I stayed during our furloughs from Africa.

> The mercy gift involves having enough compassion to actually put your hands to work and do something about it.

Bonnie had the gift of cooking, which I found to be a happy coincidence. After all, I had the gift of eating! We went to church with Kyle and Bonnie every Sunday. And every Sunday when the service was over, Kyle would find me, grab me by the arm, and say, "Come on, son, I want to show you what a sermon looks like in action." We would climb into his old truck and drive a mile and a half down the road to the local nursing home.

To be honest, nursing home residents weirded me out back then. I didn't know what to do when they were slumped over, making strange noises, or spilling things. Kyle didn't seem to notice. He'd brush their hair and straighten their clothes. From time to time he'd climb onto the bed with them and tell them that God loved them and so did he. Kyle knew that his words and hugs brought happiness into their lives, and I believe he knew that whatever sacrifice he made to bring them this special gift was worth it. In room after room Kyle would repeat his acts of love and compassion. Kyle had the gift of mercy.

A few years ago I was visiting Southland Christian Church in Lexington,

Kentucky. The minister told the story of three women in the church who decided to reach out to "exotic dancers." Wanting to rescue the girls from their plight, these three Southland women started preparing dinners for them. Then the three women bought a house next to the place where the dancers worked and turned it into a halfway house. They encouraged the girls to come and live there, free of charge, until they could find other jobs for themselves.

> If you are a follower of Christ, the Bible says you *have* been gifted to serve the body of Christ.

The Southland women epitomized Isaiah 58:10: "If you spend yourselves in behalf of the hungry and satisfy the needs of the oppressed, then your light will rise in the darkness, and your night will become like the noonday." That's not just pity; that's sympathy with legs. That's mercy.

HOLY DISCONTENT

In 1998, I was one of ten ministers who spent three days with Bill Hybels (well-known pastor of Willow Creek Community Church) on Kawau Island off the northern coast of New Zealand. I will never forget how Bill looked me in the eye and asked, "Jeff, what is your holy discontent?"

"My holy what?"

"Your holy discontent. That thing that is wrong with the world that you will not rest until you fix."

That opened my eyes. "What is your holy discontent?" is such a great question because for most of us, our gifting coincides with our holy discontent. It is that thing that resonates most with us that, quite possibly, God has equipped us to tackle.

My holy discontent is with believers I've met who think evangelism is not that important. They are unmoved by the fact that the last time someone came to Jesus in their church was when President Reagan was in office. Now guess what my primary gift is—evangelism!

Maybe you already know your spiritual gifts. But if not, discovering your spiritual gifts can begin with the question "What is your holy discontent?" What are you dissatisfied with? What drives you crazy? What are you dying to fix or change?

Whether you *feel* like you have a gift or not is not the issue. If you are a follower of Christ, the Bible says you *have* been gifted to serve the body of Christ. God doesn't leave anyone out. "In [Christ Jesus] you have been enriched in every way—with all kinds of speech and with all knowledge—God thus confirming our testimony about Christ among you. Therefore you do not lack any spiritual gift as you eagerly wait for our Lord Jesus Christ to be revealed" (1 Corinthians 1:5-7).

When we use our gifts as God intended, "we will grow to become in every respect the mature body of him who is the head, that is, Christ. From him the whole body, joined and held together by every supporting ligament, grows and builds itself up in love, as each part does its work" (Ephesians 4:15, 16).

I can assure you, you will discover your gifts somewhere along the way. Go on then. Jump in!

GREAT AND PRECIOUS PROMISES

FOR INDIVIDUAL OR GROUP STUDY

O f course, the spiritual gifts mentioned in this chapter are not the only spiritual gifts. Others are listed in the following Scriptures: 1 Corinthians 12:7-11; Ephesians 4:11-13; and 1 Peter 4:10, 11. You (or your group) might want to consider taking this study of gifts deeper now or at another time.

1 "I believe in a sovereign God who moves the pieces of the chessboard from one place to another to accomplish his purposes. God called you to your church because there was a hole that only you, with your unique set of talents, abilities, and gifting, could fill" (p. 127). Do you agree with that statement? What implications does it reveal about God? about your church? about you?

2 What do you think your spiritual gifts are? If you don't know, a good way to discover them is by serving in some way. Note five areas in your church where you could be used as a volunteer.

3 Have you ever given thought to your "holy discontent"? Your gifting might coincide with that thing that is wrong with the world that you are dying to fix or change. How do you think God has equipped you to tackle this situation?

4 Make a list of the spiritual gifts discussed in this chapter. Jot down a brief definition of each one in your own words. Take a moment to think of how any of these seem to line up with your talents and abilities. If you are studying this book in the context of a small group, take some time to share with each other what one or two spiritual gifts you perceive that others in the group have.

CONCLUSION

WE LIVE IN A world where people do not always keep their promises. As a result, we have a difficult time taking anyone at his or her word. Our default position is one of suspicion whereby we question both the trustworthiness and the motives of anyone making a promise. With God, it's quite different. Not only does he keep his promises, but the promises God makes are all designed for our good.

Imagine how you would begin to live if you really trusted God's promise that he will always be with you. Think about the risks you'd be willing to take and the journeys you'd courageously embark on.

Consider your lack of anxiety if you earnestly believed that Jesus will care for you in the midst of even the most life-threatening situations.

What if you never worried again that you are missing out on anything—because you trust that God will always give you what you need? God has an endless supply of resources—and you have access to him!

Imagine knowing that you have been saved to live forever, that death no longer has a hold on you because Jesus already conquered it.

What confidence you could have if you believed that when you bring your requests to God, he always answers. What would it be like to live with the certainty that God hears all your prayers and, without fail, promises to release his power into the situation about which you are praying?

Think about what it means that all your sins—past, present, future—are forgiven, and the barrier that once existed between you and God has been removed.

What if you really believed that God's Holy Spirit will live inside you, strengthen you, and transform you into a new and improved person?

Finally, imagine the sense of purpose and meaning flowing through your days because you realize you have been designed and equipped by your Creator to play an important role in this universe. He has endowed you with certain gifts and abilities essential to a purpose that is good for you but far greater than yourself.

What a life! This is the life that every person on the planet desperately longs for. This is the life God promises those who follow him. And with God, a promise made is a promise kept!

NOTES

CHAPTER 1

1. Information in this section was taken from Joshua Piven and David Borgenicht, *The Worst-Case Scenario Survival Handbook* (San Francisco: Chronicle Books, 1999), 54, 64, 88, 137–139.

2. http://www.blueletterbible.org/lang/lexicon/lexicon.cfm?strongs=H399&t=NIV.

3. Ruth Harms Calkin song "My God Is So Big," http://www.higherpraise.com/Lyrics4/MyGodIsSoBig.htm.

4. Muhammad Ali, http://www.posterrevolution.com/gallery/enlarge.cfm?pic=pr/1/554896f.jpg. Quote taken from www.brainyquote.com.

5. Ravi Zacharias, *Cries of the Heart: Bringing God Near When He Feels So Far* (Nashville, TN: Word Publishing, 1998), 78.

CHAPTER 2

1. Billy Graham, *Hope for Each Day* (Nashville, TN: Thomas Nelson, 2002), 31.

2. Carole King song "You've Got a Friend," from the album *Tapestry,* 1971, Warner Brothers.

3. I first learned of this distinction in 1997 when I heard Dr. Tim Keller discuss the two distinct personality types exhibited by the two sisters, Mary and Martha. This narrative took on new meaning and helped me see how Jesus cares for each person in a way that is uniquely felt by each individual.

4. Some information in this section was taken from "A Saintly Woman," John Harvard's Journal, July–August 1982, http://harvardmagazine.com/sites/default/files/Mother%20Teresa-Class-Day-82 .pdf and http://www.servelec.net/mothertheresa.htm. I heard Ravi Zacharias tell the main part of the story.

5. *The Expositor's Bible Commentary,* Volume 9, Frank E. Gaebelein, general editor (Grand Rapids, MI: Zondervan Publishing House, 1981), 119.

6. Ibid.

7. en.wikipedia.org. Quote taken from http://www.monergism.com/directory/link_details/23368/Ravi-Zacharias-Sermon-Jam-Audio/c-226.

8. Some information in this section was taken from the following sources: Rene Lynch, "Son's death brings urgency to Crusade; Harvest Fellowship's youthful, rocking twist on evangelism gains somber momentum as pastor vows to go on," *Los Angeles Times,* August 2, 2008, California, Part B, Metro Desk, B2. Also "Evangelist tells 109,000 faith carried him when son died," http://www.wnd .com/?pageId=72784#ixzz1KYudy6MR and http://www.harvest.org/crusades/2008/anaheim. I also spoke with people who attended the event.

CHAPTER 3

1. Bonnie L. Gracer, "What the Rabbis Heard: Deafness in the Mishnah," *Disability Studies Quarterly,* Spring 2003, Vol. 23, No. 2, http://www.dsq-sds.org.

2. Ibid.

3. Ibid.

4. *The Revell Bible Dictionary* (Grand Rapids, MI: Fleming H. Revell, 1990, second printing 1994), 503, 875.

5. http://www.sermoncentral.com/illustrations/sermon-illustration-richard-jones-stories-purpose-covet-commandments-1020.asp.

6. Ibid.

7. Harold Abrahams character in the movie *Chariots of Fire*. Quote taken from http://www.imdb.com/character/ch0016123/quotes.

8. Jim Elliot, http://www2.wheaton.edu/bgc/archives/faq/20.htm.

9. Corrie Ten Boom, http://www.corrietenboom.com/history.htm.

CHAPTER 4

1. http://www.suffering.net/cross.htm.

2. "Calvary," www.netbiblestudy.com/00_cartimages/calvary.pdf.

3. www.dictionary.com.

4. Seneca quote taken from http://ordinand.wordpress.com/2010/01/04/seneca-can-anyone-be-found-who-would-willingly-die-on-a-cross.

5. Information in this section was taken from Gary Mihoces, "10 Hardest Things to Do in Sports," *USA Today,* Parts 1, 2, and 3; February 18–March 3, 2003.

6. J. I. Packer, his chapter in *Good Questions on Right & Wrong* (Cincinnati, OH: Standard Publishing, 2011), 8.

7. Dallas Willard, "Live Life to the Full," http://www.dwillard.org/articles/artview.asp?artID=5.

CHAPTER 5

1. Information in this chapter, regarding the Jeff Miller story, was taken from http://www.ruforhim2.com/?p=12 and http://www.dailyherald.com/article/20110124/business/799999881/print.

2. Peter Kreeft, quoted by Lee Strobel, *The Case for Faith* (Grand Rapids, MI: Zondervan, 2000), 67.

CHAPTER 6

1. There are variations in versions of this story. I've discussed this story with Ravi Zacharias. He tells it in *Jesus Among Other Gods* (CD message, Ravi Zacharias International Ministries, Norcross, GA). The story seems to have come from an article titled "Could You Have Loved This Much?" by Bob Considine (*Reader's Digest,* April 1966) and is referenced at http://www.angelfire.com/tx2/rainbow11/love.html and in *In His Everlasting Arms* by Gail MacDonald (Ventura, CA: Regal, 2000), 140–141.

2. I must give Andy Stanley credit for popularizing this idea, a line of reasoning he often uses.

3. Information in this section was taken from the *Encyclopedia of World Biography,* "Charles Blondin," http://www.notablebiographies.com/supp/Supplement-A-Bu-and-Obituaries/Blondin-Charles.html and Tony Campolo, *Let Me Tell You a Story,* (Nashville, TN: Thomas Nelson, 2000), 80.

4. Information in this section was taken from http://www.holocaustresearchproject.org/ghettos/wiesenthal.html; http://students.cis.uab.edu/tiff88/sunflower.html; http://en.wikipedia.org/wiki/Nazi_hunter; http://en.wikipedia.org/wiki/Simon_Wiesenthal; Ravi Zacharias, *Cries of the Heart,*

91–92; Simon Wiesenthal, *The Sunflower* plus symposium, revised and expanded edition (New York: Schocken Books, 1997), front matter.

5. Lorraine Hansberry, *A Raisin in the Sun* (New York: Vintage Books/Random House, 1994), 145. Quote taken from http://www.goodreads.com/author/quotes/3732.Lorraine_Hansberry.

CHAPTER 7

1. Thomas Chalmers, sermon titled "The Expulsive Power of a New Affection," http://www.covenant-reformed.org/apps/blog/show/prev?from_id=4671625. Personal info at http://www.britannica.com/EBchecked/topic/104778/Thomas-Chalmers.

2. Read more about this at: http://www.justice.gov.za/trc/index.html and http://www.beyondintractability.org/essay/reconciliation and http://www.pbs.org/pov/tvraceinitiative/facingthetruth and http://being.publicradio.org/programs/truth/inauguration.shtml.

CHAPTER 8

1. *The Expositor's Bible Commentary,* Volume 10, 129.

2. http://www.blueletterbible.org/lang/lexicon/lexicon.cfm?strongs=G4394.

3. http://www.blueletterbible.org/lang/lexicon/lexicon.cfm?strongs=G3870.

4. http://www.blueletterbible.org/lang/lexicon/Lexicon.cfm?strongs=G1653.

ABOUT THE **AUTHOR**

JEFF VINES is senior pastor of Christ's Church of the Valley in San Dimas, California. He previously served as teaching pastor at Savannah Christian Church in Savannah, Georgia. Prior to that he spent twenty years on the mission field (in Zimbabwe and New Zealand), planting churches and training leaders. For seven years he was the featured speaker on the weekly television broadcast *Questions for Life,* and frequently debated agnostics and atheists on national radio. Jeff and his wife, Robin, have two children, Delaney and Sian.

Other books by Jeff Vines:
Dinner with Skeptics (College Press)
Unleashed (contributing writer; Standard Publishing)

Find out more about Jeff at www.jeffavines.com and listen to his messages at www.ccvsocal.com and via the Call on Jesus app available at www.callonjesus.com.

Dig *deeper*
into the Word of God

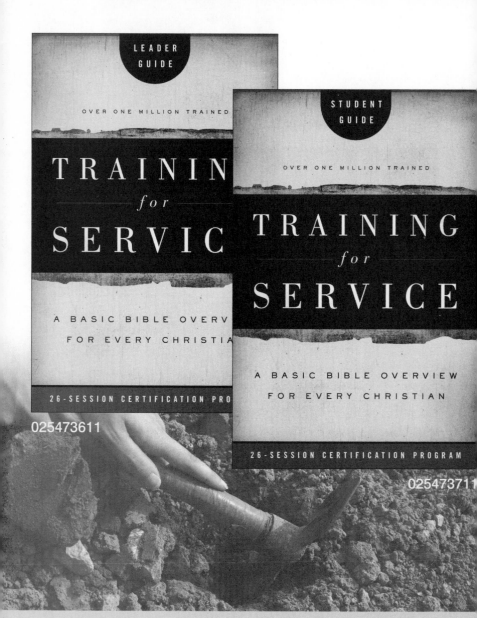